The Competitive Edge II

The Competitive Edge II
Moving Up the Levels

By Max Gahwyler
Cartoons by Patricia Peyman Naegeli

Half Halt Press
Middletown, Maryland

The Competitive Edge II: *Moving Up the Levels*
© 1992 Max Gahwyler

Published in the United States of America by
Half Halt Press, Inc.
6416 Burkittsville Road
Middletown, MD 21769

Designed by Clara Graves
Cartoons by Patricia Peyman Naegeli
Technical drawings by Clara Graves

AHSA tests and excerpts from tests reproduced with
the kind permission of the American Horse Shows
Association, Inc.

Library of Congress Cataloging-in-Publication Data

Gahwyler, Max, 1923-
    The competitive edge II : moving up the levels / by Max
Gahwyler ; cartoons by Patricia Peyman Naegeli.
        p. cm.
    ISBN 0-939481-30-8 : $25.95
    1. Dressage—Competitions. 2. Dressage tests. I. Title.
II. Title: Competitive edge 2.
SF309.6.G34 1992
798.2'4—dc20   92-39913
                                                            CIP

Contents

The quotations found throughout this book are taken from the works listed below. These are a only a part of the wealth of literature available to the serious equestrian.

Advanced Techniques of Riding, *German National Equestrian Federation,* Half Halt Press, Inc., Middletown, MD, 1986.

Classical Principles of the Art of Training Horses, *Nuno Oliveira,* Howley & Russell, Caramet, Australia, 1983.

The Complete Training of the Horse and Rider, *Alois Podhajsky,* Doubleday & Co., New York, NY, 1967.

Horsemanship, *Waldemar Seunig,* Doubleday & Co., New York, NY, 1956.

Reflections on Equestrian Art, *Nuno Oliveira,* J.A. Allen, London, UK, 1976.

Schooling Young Horses, *Werner Storl,* Breakthrough Publications, Inc., Ossining, NY, 1990.

Understanding Equitation, *Col. Jean Saint-Fort Paillard,* Doubleday & Co., New York, NY 1974.

Many horses are put under saddle much too young resulting in incurable damage to their backs and haunches, since due to their not yet completed development they are not yet capable to accommodate safely the requirements made on them. The age at which Dressage should be started in a Warmblood horse depends on the climatic conditions of his geographic area of upbringing and is six or seven years of age, and under certain circumstances eight years.

Francois Robichon de la Guérinière (1729)
(Translated by the Author)

The need for time cannot be refuted by false successes which only go to prove the opposite. For even if it is possible to train a horse up to High School at the age of eight years, at the age of ten years the so-called dressage horse would be completely worn out and useless. The principles of classical art cannot be undermined by a singular phenomenon. On the contrary, such a display merely proves that personal vanity and the desire to show off will in no way contribute to the development of the art. If the time of training is ruthlessly reduced it will lead only to a general lowering of the standard, to a caricature of the various movements, and to premature wearing out of the horse. Nature cannot be violated.

Alois Podhajsky,
Complete Training of the Horse and Rider, (1967)

Introduction

The predecessor to this book, **The Competitive Edge**, aimed to provide an introduction to competitive dressage by focusing on the lower levels. My aim in this volume is to provide some helpful considerations of what the next step entails for those who want to move from Training, First and Second levels, to Third and up to the FEI levels. It is my hope to encourage riders to look at the tests and the progression of them in a different light, rather than just riding the test movements.

But writing such a book is more difficult and certainly more controversial than offering some advice on how to get started in competitive dressage. As with everything in riding, there are

different theories and approaches and I'm sure that there will be some criticism and exception made to what follows in these pages. Nevertheless, the paucity of riders and horses out of the vast pool of dressage riders that accomplish this transition successfully make it abundantly clear to me that there is a fundamental lack of understanding or thought given to what is entailed.

This is *not* intended as a book on how to ride dressage; there are already many excellent publications available to help you with the technical skills and details. And, it is hoped, you are working with a qualified instructor.

If this book may help in some way the progressing amateur to get a better understanding of and to think through the problems ahead, the notes have accomplished their purpose. I dedicate this book to them, the segment of American dressage riders who deserve all the attention to make progress and need all the help they can muster, while actually getting very little help and encouragement.

1:
Historical Background of Competitive Dressage

Have you ever wondered why you see so many German and European warmbloods in competitive dressage? And why they seem tailor-made for the criteria and requirements in the upper levels? Why do the Germans always win in international competition? There are several good reasons for this phenomena and, once we understand them we might just stop fussing about it and go with the trend. It makes no sense to try to change the present rules and concepts to suit Thoroughbreds or other breeds even though it has been suggested quite often.

How did we get to this state of affairs? A little bit of historical background will explain how we arrived at this point today.

We don't have to go as far back as Xenophon, a figure with a fundamental understanding and approach to horses that is very close to our present-day way of thinking. Xenophon was a master of making useful, all purpose and cross-country cavalry mounts. It is interesting to speculate what he would think of present day Three Day Competition at the top levels.

Examining equestrian history between 1500 and 1850, we

learn that more and more basic schooling became prevalent, initially for military riding. However, as the Renaissance was a period of enormous artistic creativity and expression, this was reflected also in the riding where *academic equitation*, as it was then called, became an endeavor unto itself and for itself, and less and less connected to utilitarian and military objectives. In addition, the invention of the printing press for mass producing books instead of copying them by hand made distribution of thoughts on riding feasible and accessible as never before. One of the first in this field is from Grisone of Naples in 1560, and dealt with the training of the horse. This is generally considered the true beginning of modern day dressage.

However, the development was not a very smooth path and false or unsuccessful directions and methods were sometimes employed, misunderstandings occurred, and misconceptions and excesses were just as frequent and widespread as some of the divergent ideas about what is right and what is wrong of today.

Nevertheless, there was a continuous progress from the day of Grisone, Caracciola and Pignatelli of Naples in 1552, to their pupils Lohneysen in Germany, Blundeville in England, and de la Broue in France, a progress that introduced the School of Naples and its concept to their individual countries. Later came Pluvinel, instructor of French kings, who founded the *Ecole de Versaille* under Louis XIII. Pluvinel's book appeared in 1640 and is a milestone in the development of academic equitation. It is interesting to note that the books of la Broue and Pluvinel are quite close to our present-day approaches to developing the best in natural ability, while maintaining the spirit of the horse. They probably represent the best that came out of the School of Versaille or later the *Ecole des Tuilleries*.

This progress, however, was lost again by Newcastle, who published his book of riding instruction and training of the horse in English in 1743. He used much more forceful methods which represented a return to the more brutal days of the Middle Ages. However, some of Newcastle's theory and concepts were fresh, imaginative and helpful. Even Steinbrecht and de la Guérinière refer to him quite often, specifically referring to Newcastle's concept that lateral work, when done correctly is extremely helpful to the training of the horse.

Of course, we ride today quite differently than in those days; what we understand today as aids are something nobody even dreamed about then. Those were the days of often enormous bits, more a handicap or a decoration than a useful influence, and the saddle with a high pommel and cantel leading to stretched-through knees with legs pointing forward. Enormously long spurs attached to the heel were rarely used by competent riders but often formed an important part of the "image." Needless to say, under such circumstances the leg, rein, seat or spur aids as we understand them simply were not physically possible. Look at any old print from this period and you see immediately what is so fundamentally different from what we consider a correct seat and aids today.

After Pluvinel, riding became more academic and theoretical than practical, with divergent ideas and concepts and eternal bickering between the proponents of one approach or another. The English, who were initially quite taken by the academic equitation and had a great interest in this type of riding, gave it up entirely and went back to fox hunting cross-country in any style or concept as long as they could stay on top of the horse and have a good time. This state of affairs in England has not changed much up to the present; dressage riding, quite prominent now in England, is of relatively recent origin. Even today it has not reached the level of acceptance as on the continent and there was never a British school of dressage riding as in other European countries. It is somewhat analogous to what was happening in America at the same time. Certainly, England had no influence on the formation of modern dressage.

After Pluvinel, we find the most important figure in the history of dressage riding, Francois Robichon de la Guérinière (1688-1751), who worked in the Academy of the Tuilleries, the continuation of the Ecole de Versaille. It was this man who with amazing clarity crystalized the most positive aspects and accomplishments of the previous centuries into a clear, logical and very effective system of training a horse, discarding excessive and unworkable theories. Not just ultimately for the *Haut Ecole* was de la Guérinière famous, but also for the training of cross-country horses, cavalry horses, hunting and other military purposes. Without his writings we would never understand what really was accomplished in the sixteenth and seventeenth centuries. His two books, *Ecole de Cavalerie* and *Elemens de la Cavalerie*, are all encompassing equestrian guides.

De la Guérinière's contribution still in use today is the flat dressage saddle, which allowed an effective natural seat, with

legs flexed at the knee, and the feet under the rider in a supple
and relaxed fashion. This allowed for leg aids as we understand
them today. Gone were the days of stretched out legs, far ahead
of the rider and the center of gravity. A close facsimile of the
saddle introduced by de la Guérinière is still used today in the
Spanish Riding School in Vienna and at Saumur in France.
Anyone who has ever ridden in one can attest to the superb
comfort they provide, automatically allowing the rider to sit in
a natural relaxed fashion.

In addition, because of de la Guérinière's understanding and
clear objectives of what he wanted in a horse, he understood the
misconceptions and dangers of leg-yielding as introduced by
Newcastle. De la Guérinière replaced leg-yielding in his training with the shoulder-in, the cornerstone of modern dressage
training and essential for collection and suppling. Even so, our
present FEI definition is quite different from the original one of
de la Guérinière. In short, he developed the shoulder-in and
progressively pushed it to an almost forty-five degree angle,
with the inside hindleg moving under the center of gravity of
horse and rider, flexing the hocks and carrying more weight.

De la Guérinière not only synthesized, condensed and ar-
ranged the best of all the concepts of the past and put it in to an
easily understandable teaching program, he also provided
future generations with a new concept of the saddle with the
result of effective aids and, lastly, the most useful exercise in
dressage training, the shoulder-in. He is simultaneously the
culmination and end point of the academic equitation of the
sixteenth to eighteenth centuries, as well as the beginning point
of modern dressage.

What de la Guérinière accomplished can be seen today in the
Spanish Riding School in Vienna, which is based entirely on his
teachings.

The end of the dominance of the *Ecole de Versaille* and French
riding came in the French Revolution. Noblemen skilled in
academic equitation went to the guillotine and the horses most
likely ended up in a "Boucherin de Cheval," still common in
France. The heritage of that great institution was lost, and
France never recovered or was able to develop a fundamentally
coherent concept of riding and training up to our present time.
Certainly there were outstanding riders in the Cavalry School
such as Baucher, Raabe, L'Hotte, d'Aure, Decarpentry, Liçart,
and others. But much of their time was consumed in contradict-

ing each other or reexplaining the French method. On the other hand, they developed cavalry suitable to modern warfare and far removed from the concept of riding as an art for art's sake. Even today, French dressage riders have not been very prominent in international competition; the influence of France after de la Guérinière on present-day competitive dressage is therefore rather marginal.

An area where academic equitation was preserved to some extent was in Spain and Portugal, where the Andalusian horses were particularly gifted for this type of work. The use of horses in mounted bullfighting required not only agile but also well-trained horses of great elegance in their performance. From many outstanding riders, such as the Marquess of Marialva, Fernandez de Andrade, Mestre Miranda, and Diogo di Bragança, perhaps the best known exponent of our own time was Nuno Oliveira, a truly accomplished equestrian. But this Spanish influence had relatively little effect on the other side of the Pyrenees.

The French Revolution and the political rearrangement of Europe with its almost continuous war, followed by the devastation and impoverishment of the continent after the Napoleonic era, led to the almost total disappearance of academic equitation as an endeavor for its own purposes, except in the Spanish Riding School in Vienna. Furthermore, developments in military strategy required a complete rethinking of the function of the cavalry. In the eighteenth century, King Frederic II of Prussia requested that General von Seydlitz, a great horseman, redefine the training and capability of the German mounted troops. The three basic objectives von Seydlitz introduced were: speed and endurance, allowing rapid displacement of troops over great distances as a tactical advantage; a certain amount of obedience and maneuverability in order to ride in formation and to allow for easy handling of the mounts (referred to as the Campaign School, encompassing basic training but not more than Second or Third Level of today); and cross-country ability, including jumping, swimming and the ability to be sure-footed uphill and downhill, even in mud. These three objectives are very close to those developed by Xenophon for the same purpose.

The concepts introduced by the German General, von Seydlitz are the direct basis of the modern "military," or Three-Day, competition. Other countries, after being badly beaten by the new German cavalry, adopted similar reforms, and academic equitation was again forgotten.

The art of riding deteriorated as no solid basis existed any longer, a fact recognized by the leading German officers in the various cavalry schools. A movement developed in the late eighteenth and early nineteenth centuries to consolidate, stream-line and improve the teaching and training of horses and rider. This movement had the full support of the German Kaiser.

One of these officers was Ludwig Hunersdorf, who pub-lished his book on training horses in 1791. His book was based on the concepts of de la Broue and de la Guérinière, and was translated in 1843 for the Belgian cavalry. It established key concepts for dressage riding and was also used in France, until it was replaced later in the century with the flamboyant riding skills and style of Baucher.

Hunerdorf's concepts of a balanced seat, properly coordi-nated aids, and a respect and understanding of the horse, were far ahead of his time in Germany. In my opinion, his book ranks with those of de la Guérinière and Steinbrecht and is still excellent reading today.

What is remarkable is that in this same period of time, a group of horsemen in Germany worked in the same direction, creating within two decades the present-day German system of riding and training horses. This system followed to some extent the requirements of the old academic equitation, but was much less demanding and adjusted to the average ability of a cavalry soldier and his horse. How was this possible? It had already begun thirty years before when some reforms had been made. Then, in 1844, Louis Seeger, a former pupil of the Spanish Riding School who was in charge of the cavalry school in Berlin published his books and enforced his methods in the training of officers, particularly cavalry instructors. Simultaneously, Gustav Steinbrecht, who married Seeger's daughter, worked in the same direction; his notes and concepts were posthumously published and later supplemented by Hans von Heydebreck; *Gymnasium of the Horse* (1884) has been reedited for over 100 years, the last edition, published in 1966. This famous and important book is the bible of riding and teaching a horse, but is unfortunately unknown to many riders in the U.S.A. and is not currently available in English. It offered the most successful way to make German warmblood horses perform and top riders out of the cavalry remounts. Steinbrecht, Seeger (and Seidel), were all aware of Newcastle, Pluvinel and de la Guérinière, and

were directly influenced by the Spanish Riding School. During this same
period, an appropriate breeding program began to create horses best
suited for this type of training. While
the enlisted cavalry rode mostly
Hanoverians, Holsteiners, and related breeds, the officer corps was
more frequently mounted on
Trakheners and slightly higher-
blooded horses, many of them im-
ported from Poland along with
Anglo-Trakheners and some Anglo-
Thoroughbreds.

Since one of the objectives of the
cavalry school was to turn out large
numbers of instructors fairly easily
and, knowing the German mental-
ity, the uniformity of concept in instruction and selection of
horses according to Steinbrecht's guideline, has been assured
and maintained up to our present-day. These concepts are
condensed and abbreviated in the text of **Advanced Techniques of Riding** from the German National Equestrian Federation, published by the same publisher as this book.

> *The importance of the classic tenets
> of riding has been confirmed again
> and again throughout the centuries,
> and many older riders learned the
> basics of horsemanship from the
> almost legendary Germany Army
> Regulation Handbook (HDv. 12
> published in 1912, revised in 1926
> and 1937). In fact, today's guide-
> lines for basic schooling are still
> based on these publications.*
>
> **Werner Storl,**
> *Schooling Young Horses*, 1990

The Germans were also united in their absolute rejection of
Baucher and Fillis (actually an Englishman though considered
the epitome of the French school), and other French riders, as
well as other influences from the outside (or even occasionally
from the inside). It was Steinbrecht who created the famous
maxim, "Ride your horse straight and forward." In fairness,
however, it must be said that the French General, l'Hotte said
exactly the same thing at pretty much at the same time. However, this has never been widely recognized, so Steinbrecht gets
the credit!

The concept and methods of Seeger, Steinbrecht and
Heydebreck were further confirmed and established in the
fundamental equestrian document of the Cavalry School of
Hanover, called the *H. Dv. 12* (1912). While still available this
manual has not, unfortunately, been translated into English.

Heydebreck, the great follower of Steinbrecht and respon-
sible for the editing and adjusting of the original text, was
instrumental in having *H. Dv. 12* used by the German National

"Ride your horse forward and straighten it up." This sentence of Gustav Steinbrecht, on whose theoretical knowledge our riding instruction of today is based, should always be our guideline. A correctly ridden shoulder-in is indeed the most valuable gymnastic exercise we have. And there is no way of avoiding this exercise either in the training period or in the later work of training dressage competition horses.

Jean-Emile Bemelmans,
Dressage & CT magazine. April 1991

Equestrian Federation for the standards and definitions of dressage, from which the FEI rules were formulated in 1921. Our own ASHA dressage rules and definitions as well as those of most national federations worldwide are based on this original German document.

This is where the explanation lies for the questions posed at the beginning of this chapter: present-day competitive dressage was developed by Germans for Germans and for German-bred horses. The fundamental of *H. Dv. 12* were further developed by Heydebreck in 1912 in his book that dealt specifically with competitive dressage riding. This book is extremely interesting from a historical point of view. It refers to the various types of arena and letters that were used, though it does not refer to the origins of the present-day letters and the why's of their arrangement in our arena (an interesting question, to be sure). The German Federation's requirement of this time for an impeccable seat and aids before riders moved to higher levels prevented horse and rider combinations to move to levels beyond their own capability.

What If?

It may be fun to imagine what we would ride like today if competitive dressage had originated in countries other than Germany.

For example, if it came from Italy or England, we would still be waiting for it!

If it had come from Spain or Portugal, we would be all riding Andalusians and practicing the movements for bullfighting, and trying to emulate Nuno Oliveira. Instead of a reader at **E** and **B**, a friend could sit on the rump of the horse and whisper in our ear the test and coaching instructions—in as elegant a fashion as possible.

If competitive dressage had originated in France, we would

ride any way we wanted to, as long as it was elegant. We would be sitting on a Selle Francais and not worrying too much about collection.

And if Austria were the cradle of competitive dressage, we would all go back to the academic equitation of de la Guérinière.

Just think for a moment if competitive dressage riding had originated in Iceland, on Icelandic ponies. Or with the *rancheros* and their Paso Finos of Peru. Certainly an interesting speculation!

Classical?

Each school of riding had its own objectives, requirements, basic concept and equestrian terminology. This brings me to the question of "What is classical?" We use this catch word all the time, but I wish those who do would state clearly what they are referring to as *classical*, who said so, where and why, and why does it apply to us today? Otherwise, the term classical is nothing but a smoke screen. It sounds important, but actually leaves the uninformed reader totally in the dark as to what phase of academic equitation the speaker refers to.

For most Europeans and particularly the Germans, there is no doubt but that they are referring to Seidler, Seeger, Steinbrecht, Heydebreck and the *H. Dv. 12*, none of which, unfortunately, is available to us in English. So what are we talking about when we say here in America that we must follow "classical principles?" I truly don't know, since most of our riders and instructors haven't read or have no access to this kind of literature or training. Further, the variety of contradictory theories and methods that emerged over the last four hundred years often led to acrimonious disputes between proponents and opponents. It is no wonder it is easy to get confused and discouraged as to what is right. This confusion is often hidden behind this term *classical*, which has never been clearly defined for American use and means something different to anybody who uses it or hears it.

Why should something be called classical just because it was done in the sixteenth and seventeenth century on the one hand, or on the other hand, because our instructor tells us that this is the classical way to do it? We would be better off just to drop this expression from our riding vocabulary and instead develop a clear concept of why such differences emerged.

The Influence of Type of Horse

Most of the theories and methods were proposed by equestrians of unquestionable and outstanding talent and integrity. However, they may not be applicable or practical today or fit within FEI guidelines for competitive dressage. One of the underlying reasons for this was the type of horses used and the objectives to be accomplished by the various schools.

Looking at the sixteenth and seventeenth centuries when the Ecole de Versaille was the center of academic equitation, we find the tenets of the late Renaissance and early Baroque, *l'art pour l'art*, applied to riding. The utilitarian purpose of movements for military reasons vanished in the background. Pluvinel, de la Guérinière and their followers used relatively small, obedient horses, primarily horses with Spanish and some Arabian background such as Andalusians and Lipizanners, a type we can generally consider as the Baroque horse. They were talented for a particular type of work: relatively short, with very powerful haunches, and a naturally low croup with good hock action leading to a natural ability to collect, to come up in front, and stay in front of the rider's aids. Hardly any rein action was needed. With the enormous ability for self-carriage in these horses, the quality of absolute lightness is almost a natural result of their build. This type of horse was easy to work in the standard arena of those times, 12.6 to 36 meters. The type of horse closest to this model today is the original Lipizzaner, powerfully compact with relatively short legs and strides, easy to train, and with a wonderful attitude towards work of this type. Some more modern breeding tendencies are refining this horse and lengthening its legs, which makes it progressively less suitable for Baroque equitation and the Haute Ecole.

Historically situated between the two best known proponents of the Ecole de Versaille, Pluvinel and de la Guérinière, is the teaching of the Duke of Newcastle. His 1743 book, *A General System of Horsemanship*, was written in English and reprinted in facsmile here sometime ago is probably more well known to Americans than the other two. In it, you do not see the basic ideas such as the development of natural gaits to the best harmony of horse and rider, and soft and imperceptible aids. You might wonder if Newcastle lived on another planet, or never heard of his equestrian colleagues just a short distance

away. The explanation for this seems to be in the horses he worked with, as opposed to the type just discussed. He did not use the talented Andalusian, Spanish-type horses, but instead enormous Belgian draft horse stallions, with necks like iron and a basic attitude of "just make me do it if you can." This led to methods which we consider as too powerful and rough today. Newcastle's biggest pride was the invention of a sophisticated pulley rein in which the horse is used against himself, and results in the excessive flexion of the head Newcastle demanded. Applying the soft and sophisticated approach of training of the Ecole de Versaille which lead to collection, self-carriage and lightness, would have been totally frustrated by these animals. But using Newcastle's method on a small Andalusian stallion would probably have broken the poor horse's neck in the first session! Nevertheless, some of his theoretical concepts such as the use of lateral movements as a means of achieving collection and suppleness, and the work around the single pillar were basically correct. They ultimatly led de la Guérinière to develop the shoulder-in on up to four tracks, while pointing out the shortcomings and dangers of a simple leg-yielding. Also, many of the concepts of Newcastle were greatly appreciated by Steinbrecht; one can find them in *Gymnasium of the Horse*, from where they have found their way into the present day FEI and AHSA manuals, as well as being used in our training method.

It was the dressage of the late eighteenth and early nineteenth centuries which fundamentally determined our present-day concept of what is right and what is wrong, and the controversies and conflicting theories of the early nineteenth century are still with us today. In order to fully understand why, it is important to realize that academic equitation was primarily done at this time in and for the circus. Equestrian centers like the Ecole de Versaille under the French kings no longer existed. The German cavalry followed *H. Dv. 12*. The period of the Renaissance and Baroque gave way to a much more radical romanticism and liberalism in France, rejecting the past and striving to invent everything anew, including the training of the horse.

The most outstanding and talked about, as well as talented and controversial, figure in France of this period was Francois Baucher (1796-1873), a circus rider whose performances not only had to be accurate but also to satisfy a certain flamboyance and showmanship. The circus in this period bears no resemblance to the circus of today; it was a dramatic and glamorous affair. Flying changes every stride were Baucher's invention. The Baroque-type horses as used in the Spanish Riding School today, and related breeds such as those selected by Pluvinel and de la Guérinière for their ability to collect, were totally rejected. The British Thoroughbred was the horse of the choice of the time. Simply put, Baucher avoided the concept of putting more weight on the haunches, using instead a collection with equal distribution of weight on all four legs. To compensate for this, lightness, self-carriage and eleagance were emphasized and, in a way, Baucher achieved remarkable success. However, his methods required an exceedingly talented rider and sophisticated training which in the hands of the average equestrian or beginner were a total disaster. This polarized the French riding community with l'Hotte and Raabe of the Saumur as devoted pupils and defenders, while the Count d'Aure became his fanatical rival and antagonist. It was the concept of making a horse over by any means that was not acceptable to d'Aure. It was also in this period that the statement was first used, "When knowledge stops, brutality begins," which is just as true today as it was then.

Outside of France, Baucher was roundly rejected, primarily by Seeger, Seidel and Steinbrecht (also a trainer of circus horses). The Thoroughbred was considered unsuitable for academic equitation and, the Germans had created a dressage tailor-made for their own horses, the German warmblood. On the other hand, the Saumur and the Cadre Noir with their French Thoroughbreds, the Selle Francais, retained many of the concepts of l'Hotte, Raabe and Baucher. This can be seen when comparing pictures of identical movement, executed by the French School and by the Spanish Riding School, or present-day German riders. However, the French concept and definitions do not really conform to our present-day FEI standards as the French school was ignored when the rules were written.

A similar, exceedingly talented rider but without any lasting influence was James Fillis (b. 1834), a follower of Baucher and the French school. His outstanding book is primarily interesting from the historic point of view and the photographs of the period it includes. He too was riding almost exclusively Thoroughbreds, following Baucher, using all their natural attributes with great skill, and avoiding imitation of Lipizzaners or German warmbloods. Here again, Fillis' riding was determined by the type of horse he had available and liked best.

The Last Great Innovation

The late 19th and early 20th centuries brought not only fundamental developments such as the beginnings of competitive dressage, but even more profound changes and innovation in riding cross-country and over fences.

Frederico Caprilli revolutionized jumping over fences and natural obstacles through his basic concept of schooling, controlling and sitting with the motion of the horse on the flat and over obstacles. He is credited with the creation of the forward seat, although it is clear that some riders before him had the same idea. Even so, it was in the Italian Cavalry School headed by Caprilli at Pinerolo and the famous cross-country facility in Tor di Quinto that the modern jumping style evolved.

It is an interesting historical note that both dressage and jumping styles originated in Italy, the former with Grisone in Naples and the latter with Caprilli in Pinerolo.

In the United States, it was Vladimir Littauer, a Russian cavalry officer and Colonel D.H. Chamberlin of the U.S. Cavalry who were most instrumental in bringing the Caprilli concepts to the attention of American riders, in the years 1920 through 1940. Later, under Bert de Nemethy and William Steinkraus jumping style and technique reached unquestionable peaks, the envy as well as the example for jumper riders around the world.

I may have digressed a little bit from the basic objectives of this book, but I believe that anybody interested in moving to higher levels should have at least a superficial knowledge of the past and not be impressed by the continuous rhetoric of "classical," or of one method or another. These riders should understand the values, concepts and the reasons for their development as well as the type of horses for which they were created.

A review of important dates in the development of modern competitive dressage shows clearly just how recent a sport it is, and that it is still changing and will probably do so for some time. It was in 1912 that for the first time dressage was part of the Olympic Games. The FEI was only founded in 1921. It was in

1928 that for the first time team medals were competed for, and the modern arena and the concept of levels were introduced. It was not until 1949 that the first non-Olympic FEI Dressage Championship took place. And only in 1952 was this sport opened to non-commissioned officers, civilians and women; previously it was only military officers that were allowed to compete. Only in 1981 was the young rider category in dressage competition introduced. It was in 1985 that the World Cup for Dressage was organized with the first competition held in 1986.

So looking to the future, we can certainly expect continuous change and development to go on. We are witnessing the creation and development of a new type of equestrian sport that did not, in its present form, exist before.

2:
Of Horses, Humans and Centaurs

The Greek mythological figure of the centaur should be the most appealing image for any equestrian: the total integration of the powerful and athletic body of a horse with a human intellect as a guiding factor. This is something the very serious rider strives for, but never really achieves. This is the challenge as well as the frustration of dressage as the ideal unison of horse and human is and will always remain just a dream, only realized in the world of ancient mythological concepts. But it speaks volumes for the equestrian standards of long ago from which we can learn. It also tells us that the equestrians of those times found the same challenges, disappointments and setbacks as we do and dreamed up a marvelous solution—the centaur.

So, to move up the levels, we have to get a little closer to this ideal, a better unison between horse and rider. The responsibility, of course, being primarily the rider's.

Recent archeological findings indicate that man was riding horses and using bits as far back as 6000 years ago. Why then do we still have trouble riding and are no further ahead than our ancestors of many thousand years ago? With this long term association between man and horse, one should think homo sapiens would have developed a pat approach to riding, almost a computer program that always produces super riders and super horses. However, just the opposite is true; all you have to do is look around you at any horse show and you quickly realize there is lots of room for improvement.

So what is the problem? One of the main reasons, I think, is the fact that horses and humans are built, react, move and think totally different from each other. The horse, doing the actual work with the handicap of the rider on his back, cannot change his way of moving. Therefore, better riding is a progressive integration of the human mind and body into the movement and thinking of the horse. This becomes instantly clear if we compare the totally disorganized, and uncoordinated beginner on a horse, to an accomplished upper level rider where horse and man are in better unison in body and purpose.

Anyone who ever climbed on a horse, now or 6000 years ago, has to start at the same awkward stage and, gets only as far as she wants or physically can. That is the reason we are not further ahead today than thousands of years ago. You cannot learn riding based on someone else's experience. You must do it yourself.

It is a different feeling to move and cover ground with four legs as a horse does than to walk on your own two feet. But this is riding. Riding is motion, motion that is totally different than ours, where four legs and a horizontal body must be properly coordinated in all three gaits in a way that is totally alien to our erect way of moving.

Since perfection is not of this world, learning and improving is a lifetime proposition, with no such thing as a perfect mastery obtainable. But we can improve despite our limitations if we make a conscious effort to understand how a horse moves and functions, and then try to do something about and with it, instead of against it.

Look at things from the horse's point of view. Riding is motion and the first concern for the horse is to maintain a safe balance under all circumstances. This is achieved primarily by the automatic reflexes of equilibrium, which try to keep the center of gravity where it is always property supported. If this is not the case, there is immediately a feeling of insecurity which the horse, as well as the rider, try to correct.

With a horse, the center of gravity is never supported directly under any circumstances. The center of gravity is located in the middle of the horse and supported by four legs in the "corners." Each time the support in one corner is removed, the horse has a tendency to fall in that direction. In order to stay on his feet and balanced, the horse must shift whatever weight was on this leg to the three other legs.

What are the consequences? The horse must first compensate for this disappearance of support by shifting the previously carried weight of that leg to the two or three other legs by a variety of mechanisms. He uses a moveable part of the body, his head and neck to balance himself. Or, he moves a diagonal pair of legs so that the center of gravity is always supported by an opposite pair of legs: right front, left back, or left front and right back. Also, the more narrow a horse moves behind, the better his balance since the haunches are moving much closer to the center of gravity than when they are wide. As a matter of fact, a horse that goes wide behind has too much trouble adjusting his balance and can never develop real engagement, impulsion, or collection. A well-trained horse must move narrowly with his haunches, not only going straight forward but moving toward the center of gravity. Only this allows for true support and lightness in front.

The only gait in which the center of gravity is continuously supported by a diagonal pair of legs is the trot. Therefore, only in the trot can the head and neck carriage of the horse be absolutely quiet. If the hands of the riders remain absolutely steady, no compensation by the horse's head and neck for equilibrium are necessary. This fact was well known to the masters of academic equitation such as de la Guérinière, Newcastle and their contemporaries, as well as to riders such as Fillis who extended this concept to include the walk and considered the diagonal walk the correct walk for an educated horse and rider. It should be noted here that a diagonal walk is not an unnatural walk, since in the rein back we ask that the horse step diagonally backwards—so why not the same going forward? It would certainly be a much more logical approach to a collected walk than what we are doing today.

In the walk, however, as ridden today, the center of gravity is never directly supported. As a result, the horse consistently uses his neck and head in a combined motion up and down and left and right to compensate for one leg being off the ground while shifting the weight to the other one. This must be allowed, even if hardly perceptible, if the walk is to remain correct. If we interfere too much, the horse will begin pacing, which is for him a safer way to proceed if he is not allowed to compensate for the natural rotation of the weight. The rider must allow this motion to take place by a very feeling hand and allow the motion of the rhythm of this gait. If we "listen" to the reins, they give us a very sure indication of what is going on. But, the narrower the horse walks behind and in front, the less this motion becomes necessary and the quieter the walk appears. Pacing is always a result of incorrect aids and interference with the natural walk.

Similarly, in the canter (the most difficult gait for a horse as far as balance is concerned), this concept becomes even more critical, particularly with an incompetent rider on his back. In this four phased gait, the total weight of the horse and rider are carried from the outside hindleg at the start of the movement, rolling forward over the diagonal composed of the inside hind and outside front, to the inside leading leg which ultimately absorbs the entire weight of rider and horse in the forward motion. If the diagonal thrust of the movement continued, the horse would fall on his face. To avoid that, the horse has to transfer the entire weight of himself and the rider back to the outside hindleg. This is the fourth phase of the canter. As an aside, this explains why four beat music is easier to ride to in the canter, as opposed to three beat compositions such as the waltz. Again, this is done by using his neck and head to balance, shifting the weight from the front, and allowing the hindleg to come under and catch the weight and impulsion again.

If the rider does not allow that, the horse will canter very flat and never develop the full beauty of the canter. It is therefore essential that we allow the young horse especially, who does not yet carry the main weight on his haunches but is on his forehand, this balancing. This is done with the inside hand in a slightly giving rein with every stride, in the rhythm of the movement. Only then will the horse be capable of developing the full beauty of the gait and be unafraid of cantering forward, reaching and being more free and "up" in his movement. He will be capable of staying on the bit, correct, and remain light. He will also be able to make correct down transitions from behind, without falling on his forehand.

The Unpleasant Truth About Riding

Riders expect the horse to be ambidextrous: to become straight, equally supple to both sides, accepting the bit equally well on both sides, and having the same strengths of impulsion and support in both hindlegs. But we ourselves remain one-sided, crooked, usually with a scoliosis, a slightly tilted pelvis, one leg shorter than the other, with our head (which weighs about 25 pounds) carried to one side or the other by a bad habit, and much stronger in the right hand than in the left hand. And most riders do not do anything about it.

As a result, our influences on the horse are crooked, uneven and one-sided but, nevertheless, we expect the horse to be just the opposite. I think we have to be very aware of how *we are* physically and what *we can* do about our own bodies in order to ride better. Let's face it: the biggest handicap the horse faces in his life, preventing him from achieving his potential, is the level of incompetence of the rider of his back. Therefore, if anything goes wrong, never blame your horse. Always ask yourself what you are doing wrong. If you do not know, ask an expert's advice. He or she can probably in a very short observation period, point out some of the fundamental reasons making your riding difficult.

It is this lack of understanding of how to influence the horse in his own language and body motion that makes riders resort to a very crude system of inflicting pain, leading the horse to nothing more than trying to avoid it and, in so doing, ultimately achieving what we are asking. If you really think about it, bits, spurs, whip, draw reins, chambons, martingales, and so on are nothing more than forceful mechanisms of creating pain and discomfort.

No ballet master would teach his prima ballerina to perform better by using a whip or an iron prod to improve her dancing. I think the same should apply to riding. Very often what you see going on in the dressage arena is terrible. If horses could scream in pain, the noise in these arenas would be such that none of us would ever ride again. But the fact that horses are silent does not give us the right to abuse them, without even giving a thought to what we are doing wrong. We should always realize that punishing a horse for doing something wrong or for not understanding what we want has never taught a horse how to do right.

Acceptance of our own role in the incorrectness of the horse is the beginning of the realization of the image of the centaur.

3:
Understanding Moving Up

While it may seem an overwhelming proposition to ride Third, Fourth or even FEI levels for a beginner or someone who has been stuck at First or Second level for years, there is really nothing impossible about it. It takes an understanding of what the higher levels are all about and developing a correct sequence of priorities of how to get there. Once you get the objectives established for yourself and your horse, and a proper approach to training priorities, you will wonder why you did not do it before.

Let's have some fun moving up. And you should also let your horse have some fun, since just riding dressage day after day is not really what your horse wants or needs. If you have a nice hunt in the neighborhood, go hunting; any good dressage horse jumps well. Go cross-country or trail riding. Do whatever you want, but do not just concentrate on dressage; dressage is *your* problem, not your *horse's*. Once you understand, your horse will easily do it anyway. That, I think, is the basic secret to dressage. As a matter of fact, we see more and more excellent horses in this country but the quality of rides has not improved dramatically over recent years. This only proves the point that doing well in dressage competition is 80 percent the problem of the rider and only 20 percent of the horse. You cannot buy a score, no matter how much money you spend. *You* must earn it and you must ride yourself; whatever you achieve is yours as well as your horse's. Look at it this way: 15 to 20 years are needed to make a good Grand Prix rider but only five or six to make a Grand Prix horse. So who has to learn more, the horse or the rider? And let's not forget that the rider has to adjust to the horse, rather than the horse to the rider. That's exactly where the problem lies in moving up.

The Practical Approach to the Problems Ahead

Just wishing to move up from the lower levels and hoping it will magically happen by itself is unfortunately not the way it goes. Nor does just riding more and more make it happen. Even if you spend many hours on horseback, unless you or your instructor knows exactly what is needed at any given stage of training and how to integrate it in an effective program, you will likely be wasting your time and not achieving progress. On my own part, in order not to get lost or sidetracked, I always divided competitive dressage riding into three separate parts: objectives, methods to achieve the objectives and the test itself.

Objectives

Let's consider both long term and short term objectives.

Long Term Objectives. Obviously the ultimate long term objective is to ride at FEI Levels, preferably Grand Prix. But at the very least it is to develop the horse in a sound way to his full potential and athletic capabilities.

Short Term Objectives. Here you will have to address a specific problem or problems which if not solved prevent you from progressing effectively. Examples are making the horse straight, correct transitions or extensions, the correction of flying changes which are incorrect (i.e., late behind), and so one. Whatever your immediate objective, it must be addressed in a logical way. And as you progress, practically everything you can conceive of will sooner or later arrive on this list. If you accept that this problem must be resolved before you can move on, the next step is to figure out exactly how you will go about it. To just go ahead and ride it over and over will not be good enough any longer as it may have been at Training, First and to a certain extent, Second level.

Methods to Achieve Your Objective

Once you have identified your immediate objectives, you and your instructor must have an absolutely clear idea of how to achieve it. If it relates to a specific problem, you must have a clear idea of *how* to correct it. One of the basic principles is that if something does not work, or if you run into resistance, it is *not* the mere repetition of the same movement or gait that will solve the problem; it is by doing something much more fundamental that will ultimately lead to the solution. This is where your instructor becomes critically important. He or she must have studied the historical background of dressage riding. They should know the various concepts, theories, and approaches that have been used, illustrated, and written down over the past 400 hundred years. From this store of knowledge comes the ability to select the method to be applied appropriately to you and your individual horse in order to make progress.

It is essential to determine at the outset if the problem is more yours or if it is more the horse's. Remem-

The rider will not eliminate faults by repeating exercises unsuccessfully executed, but only by going back to the basic training.

Alois Podhajsky, *Complete Training of Horse and Rider*, 1967

ber, a good horse and a good rider can do anything. The same horse and an uneducated rider, nothing. You may find this a harsh opinion, but let's look at the some practical examples that will illustrate the point and, hopefully, help you in your progress. The goal is to help you think and analyze independently about what is needed. There is no pat system for all problems and all horses. Your instructor must be capable of individualizing a program. And you must develop an analytical and intellectual approach to this most sophisticated discipline of riding, in order not to fall into a mechanical pattern which may work for some but certainly not for all your problems.

Example 1: "My horse is crooked."

It's not just your horse. Every young horse is crooked, accepting the bit better on one side than the other, and leaning on the rider's hands. Horses have all been crooked for the last 6000 years, and every rider since then has had to deal with the problem, from the backyard pony rider to the Spanish Riding School Bereiter.

Pulling and yanking on the reins is useless and certainly not the answer, even if it is done all the time in sheer frustration. Nor is constant overbending, riding in circles or straight lines.

Why not follow the established methods of the Spanish Riding School, where the system has been refined over the last four hundred years on the young stallions (called *Abdruecken*)? Consider what Colonel Podhasky has to say about it.

You might also be consoled by the fact that the young Lipizzaner stallions are just as crooked as your horse, at least in the beginning of their careers!

Example 2: "My horse's half pass flows well to his hollow side but is often difficult to the other."

Here, repetition and using force definitely makes things much worse. Three hundred years ago, de la Guérinière found the same problem

Only the straightened horse will enable the rider to carry out the thorough physical training which will be required if the highest standard is to be reached in the art of equitation. All serious books on riding stress this point: "Straighten your horse and ride him forward." I should like to amplify this sentence with: "Only when your horse is straight can he go forward with impulsion and harmony."

...Crookedness of the horse ought to be the nightmare of every honest rider.

Alois Podhajsky, *Complete Training of the Horse and Rider*, 1967

when he was training his horses. Let's read what he has to say about it.

Example 3: "My horse is late behind in his flying changes."

This is a common problem, seen all the time. Again, repetition only makes it worse by reaffirming the faulty techniques. Think about it. Here's a hint: the real problem is that the horse has never been taught to canter straight and from behind.

Let's analyze the problem and most likely source. Horses that have been taught mostly to canter from the trot (which originates in front) associate the aids to the canter on with the front legs. Hence, the aids for the flying change produce the change in front first, ahead of the hindlegs, instead of originating from behind as should be.

So you must reschool your horse to associate your aids to begin the canter from the haunches. You must go back and teach your horse walk to canter, canter to walk, halt to canter, and canter to halt transitions. In order to teach your horse to canter straight from the walk, use the shoulder-fore as a starting position, which helps the inside hindleg to stay engaged.

Once your horse understands this, the changes will not only be straight but will come from behind.

It is obviously much easier to do this right from the beginning rather than wait until you run into trouble

> ... *In the previous chapter we said that the shoulder-in right works on the right shoulder and therefore is a preparation for lateral work to the left.*
>
> *Through shoulder-in right you progress to the half pass to the left.*
>
> *If a horse refuses to step laterally to one side, we have the proof that it has not yet been sufficiently exercised in the shoulder-in to the other.*
>
> **de la Guérinière,**
> *Ecole de Cavalerie,* 1729
> (Translated by the author)

with flying changes. Your horse should have been taught to canter on from the walk or halt very early in his training, and certainly well before Second Level.

But remember, we are in good company here with Podhasky, Oliveira, Steinbrecht and other authorities who have all faced exactly the same problem.

This list of examples could be extended on and on, but the point I wish to make is that you must directly approach these problems, not just avoid them or ride by the seat of your pants hoping they will fix themselves. By repeating them over and over you'll get nowhere, but by approaching them in a logical, analytical way, by going back to basic gymnastics, you will solve them. Only then are you beginning to ride dressage and enjoy and understand the most sophisticated aspect of this equestrian sport. Without it, dressage remains mechanical.

With this logical approach, dressage may become real art and a true integration of horse and rider and, for a few gifted horse and rider combinations, a real artistic endeavor.

However, you have lots and lots of help in solving your problems. Generation upon generations of rider have found the same problems and have put their findings down in writing

available to you today. Why not benefit from their experiences, their humiliations and frustrations as well their achievements and successes? It is at this stage, when you are seriously interested in moving up, that the time has come to spend your winter evenings reading some of the literature that has evolved over the past centuries.

In this sense, dressage riding is extremely encouraging because the problems you face have already been faced by much better riders and, in most instances, solved. It will be your fundamental understanding and the knowledge you gain from the literature that will help you solve your problems.

The Test Itself

Dressage tests have only one purpose: to allow a knowledge-able judge to get an accurate assessment of the correctness and deficiencies of your horse and your riding at any given stage of training in roughly five minutes. Nothing else.

Tests are not designed to teach the horse anything. They are composed solely to demonstrate instantly shortcomings and strong points and should never be an objective by and in themselves. Therefore, always remember that since the test do not teach your horse anything, simply programming your horse for a given test or competition will not lead very far in training for advancement.

A well-judged test should tell the competitor what he did well and what he should do to progress further. It should never be just a list of mistakes and negative comments. A test sheet should distinguish clearly between those mistakes and good points made by the rider and those made by the horse.

The key to every test is always the definition and objectives printed on the cover, and the directive ideas for every move-ment. That is the basis of performance and judging.

In the lower levels such as Second or Third level, roughly 50 percent of the tests are technical movements and 50 percent are movements of gaits. As you move up, though, the distinction between those two becomes more fluid and combined so that by the time you ride Grand Prix, all movements are highly technical with a quality of gait that allows for no relaxation or mistakes.

All tests are symmetrical. Unless your horse is perfectly straight, equally supple with equal freedom in both shoulders and with equally powerful haunches with driving and support-ing capability, you will never exceed 60 percent in your score. The concept in the old USDF freestyle tests that movements had only to be executed to one side was a fundamental misconcep-tion of what dressage is all about.

As you move up the levels, coefficients for key movements are abundant and it will be the execution of those movements that will have the greatest effect on your success or frustration. They not only affect your score for the movement, but also influence the collective marks. So when analyzing or selecting a test for your next competition, be certain those movements having coefficients are within the ability of your horse in order to make 7's or 8's.

Take the tests for what they are, namely, *testing exercises*, and enter the levels where you and your horse are competent and comfortable. It is much better to ride a lovely Prix St. George than a miserable Intermediate II. You and your horse will be much happier leaving the ring after having done a good test at a slightly lower level than what you are working on at home than struggling through a test at a level where things are not yet working correctly.

4:
The Aids

Moving up the levels requires a more sophisticated and developed understanding of the principles of the aids than was acceptable before. Analyzed individually, the aids are simple, clear and easily understood by practically all horses and easily used by any rider. The difficulty comes in when progressively more advanced movements require the proper coordination of aids in a consistent and clear manner.

This, however, is possible only if horse and rider connect at a solid base, that is, in a relaxed, quiet steady seat at all gaits. Without this connection, moving to higher levels is impossible as there is no central point from where our aids emanate, either by themselves or in a coordinated fashion. Without a steady seat as the base, we give unplanned and uncoordinated signals, pushes and changes of weight which only confuses the horse and never makes him really understand. We must never forget that it is impossible for a horse to distinguish between unintentional aids, those signals and influences by the rider due to lack

The sophistication of the rider is clearly demonstrated by his seat and his influence and effectiveness. The quieter and more effective and invisible these aids are, the higher the equestrian skill of the rider.

Not the stiff, rigid upper body position, but the soft incorporation into the motion of the horse is the hallmark of a good seat. ...In judging a dressage test, the seat of the rider becomes a determining factor.

Hans von Heydebreck,
Die Deutche Dressurprufung, 1929
(Translated by the author)

Above all he (the rider) will strive to prevent any unintentional changes of weight, as these are the gravest mistakes to be committed!

... The aids by weight are the most refined of all influences. Used unilaterally, they affect the position of the haunches, and bilaterally, they put the horse straight .... Putting the weight in the outside stirrup induces the horse to move laterally.

de la Guérinière,
Ecole de Cavalerie, 1729
(Translated by the author)

of balance and unsteady seat, or shifting legs or poor hands, from those aids deliberately executed with a clear objective in mind. Those unintentional aids lead to a progressive dulling of the horse's response and even so-called resistance, which is exactly the opposite of what correct training tries to achieve. Improving this is not the horse's responsibility but is entirely the rider's. However, more often than not, the horse is blamed for being resistant and unresponsive instead of the rider for lack of skill. Remember, in dressage we want a maximum response with a minimum of aids and not the opposite. This is completely the responsibility of the rider.

Weight, Seat and the Center of Gravity

A well trained horse responds to the slightest shift of weight. Weight is the most sophisticated, invisible and effective aid. It relates directly to the most fundamental automatic reflexes of a horse—staying on his feet and being balanced.

A horse always follows the rider's weight—to the right or left, forward or backward, to bring the center of gravity back where it is comfortable. Therefore, by shifting your weight to the left, you make the horse follow you to the left.

School horses or horses ridden by beginners learn to disregard this influence completely as the rider never sits where she should be, bouncing around and shifting weight constantly. Our aim is to develop sensitivity to the weight aids, and to develop the positive effects from clear and consistent application.

Whatever the movement, a circle, a corner, a half pass, or a pirouette, the rider should always be ahead of the horse and take the horse with her—not pulling or kicking a horse in one direction while still leaning into the other. It is similar to jumping a course where you look where you are going: at the next obstacle, while the horse is still going over the fence. The horse will follow you because the simple act of looking changes your position by at least 20 to 30 pounds in the new direction, which is a clear indication to the horse where you want to go. Imagine you are carrying a heavy backpack and it shifts to one side. You would automatically step back under the weight to regain your equilibrium and put the center of gravity where it is more comfortable. This is exactly what the horse does if you allow him to. The expressions used to make this clear to the student all mean the same thing: "the horse follows your eyes;" "put more weight in the stirrup on one side;" "sit on the left seatbone;" or "take your shoulder back on the inside." Good riders know this from either a theoretical point of view, or simply by the practical experience of riding well.

If you start from the beginning to teach a young horse to listen to your weight, by the time you reach Third Level this aid becomes more and

The rider who is not properly in the saddle, supple, and as one with the horse can never achieve any independence between the various aids, a condition sine qua non *to insure good hands.*

Nuno Oliveira, *Classical Principles of the Art of Training Horses,* 1983

When the weight of the body is transferred into the direction of the lateral movement, it will support the effect of the outside leg because the horse will try to step under the centre of gravity of the rider

Alois Podhajsky, *Complete Training of Horse and Rider,* 1967

The spur should be used only in an advanced stage of training, and only when required to reinforce the pushing aids. The use of the spur is the last resort and, as with other things in life, the last resort should be reserved for emergencies. The spur should touch the horse's side with an increased pressure of the leg and the application should be discontinued the moment the aid has obtained the required result. The spur should never be used sharply as an aid, because it would then no longer be an aid but a punishment.

Alois Podhajsky, *Complete Training of Horse and Rider*, 1967

more imperceptible to any onlooker. It is an exquisite way to guide your horse from movement to movement, in a perfect understanding between rider and horse. It also obviates any dramatic or excessive leg aids which are only needed when you have contradictory aids.

The Educated Leg

With your weight aids working correctly, your leg aids become much less strenuous and more effective, particularly if you use them for the natural movement of the gait and not against it. For a horse to move a hindleg more forward or under himself is possible only when this leg does not carry any weight, that is, when it is swinging forward off the ground. Once the leg is placed on the ground and carrying between 400 and 800 pounds of weight, the horse cannot respond, even if you use 3-inch spurs with sharp rollers. Constant tapping, or using your leg or spur at the wrong moment, is counterproductive, senseless, irritating and dulling to the horse, who actually is being kicked off the bit. The timing of your aids is, therefore,

critical. The rider must understand the mechanics and kinetics of the horse in order to teach him to respond and to not create a problem by incorrect aids. Remember, though, that you can only have an educated leg used in the rhythm of the movement if your seat is correct: natural, relaxed, smooth, and not digging into the back of your horse at every stride.

Good Hands

Good hands are quiet hands. The hands are the first line of communication between horse and rider and indicate immediately if something is amiss.

Consider this: when you lunge your horse, putting side reins on the snaffle and the lunge line on the cavesson, the horse adjusts obediently and easily to the frame asked for. The horse adjusts the pressure in his mouth himself. Note that attaching a lunge line to the bit is a clear sign of equestrian ignorance and the lack of any basic understanding what lunging is all about. The key point here is that once the horse adjusts to the side reins, nobody is pulling back further if he gives. Therefore, think of your hands as an attachment of side reins. Ask for a frame but once the horse adjusts, never pull back further, see-saw, or wiggle your fingers. How can a horse stay on the bit if you continually yank around on the reins, move your hands, or give useless, incorrect and ineffective half halts for no good reason? Why should the horse have any confidence in your hands under those circumstances? Being on the bit reflects the trust of the horse in the rider's hands. Never intentionally or unintentionally abuse this confidence or you will never feel what it means to ride a horse that is really with you.

Only once this natural confidence is developed can a soft closing of the fingers be effective, or a half halt go through. As long as the horse is defensive because of your unsteady hands, nothing works. Again, your hands can only be quiet, independent and receptive if your seat is quiet and confirmed. You cannot use your reins as a means to steady yourself in the saddle or to demand collection in front without getting it from behind. Frankly, before we learn to use our hands intelligently, we must learn *not* to use them. This is hard, very hard and difficult—but essential.

None of these aids used individually will ever produce a movement such as a shoulder-in, flying change, or a pirouette. In real life, moving up to the higher levels is a progressive sophistication in coordinating the fundamental aids in an infinite variety of combinations and shades depending on the movement or transition you want, the responsiveness, and the training of your horse. Moving up beyond Second Level depends more on your improving your aids than training of the horse. You should not even try to teach your horse more advanced work if your aids are not in place.

The following table ranking the use of aids might make it a little bit clearer what a major change is happening at, approximately, between Second and Third Levels.

Young Rider, First or Second Level:
1. Reins
2. Voice
3. Heels, legs, spur
4. Whip, seat, weight, balance

Advanced Rider, Third Level and Up
1. Seat, balance, weight, center of gravity
2. Legs
3. Reins
4. Spur and whips

The Consistency of Training

It is essential to use the same aids in the early training of the horse so as never to confuse him. This will also give a solid basis on which to fall back when needed. It is the use of your leg in the rhythm of the horse to gain impulsion, your seat, weight and your quiet hands, and the sophisticated combination of all of them which will result in progressively more complicated movements. What need is there to teach a horse leg-yielding if he has already learned to respond to your leg correctly, when very shortly he will learn a correct half pass?

Why should your horse have to canter by being kicked on the outside, throwing him over his inside shoulder and cantering crookedly if he needs to learn later just the opposite, if you ever want to canter correctly? Why not teach your horse from the beginning to canter right from the walk? And from a shoulder-fore position in order to make him understand that the leg aids are related to the impulsion from the back? When you teach him flying changes later, he will associate your aids with the haunches and not with the front end, therefore never changing late behind and cantering straight.

The more consistent your aids are from the beginning, the easier it will be to move your horse up, provided you and your instructor know exactly how to go about in a progressive, constructive way that never demands an abrupt change in technique. Obviously, for the horse, the transition from Second to Third Level is no problem, whereas the progressive sophistication of the aids becomes the responsibility of the rider.

Besides these fundamental aids, there are other ways to communicate with your horse, such as the tension or relaxation of your back, your voice, or the friendly pat on the neck when all is going well. At the other end are your spurs and whip as a reinforcement of the other aids. These, however, are only appropriate when used to support the other, natural aids, never as means to cruelty and punishment.

In the lower levels, the size of the spur is directly proportional to the incompetence of the rider.

5:
The Big Step Up

The biggest step forward we ask of the horse is to move from the basic working gaits to true dressage training, beginning in Second Level. True dressage training requires as absolute basics such qualities as engagement, impulsion, self-carriage—all of which are only possible on a straight horse.

So let's take a look at this too-often forgotten concept of riding straight. Why this emphasis on riding and developing a truly straight horse, you may ask, when there is not a single movement in the tests that says "straight"? Straightness is not even prominently mentioned in the definition of the higher ASHA or FEI Levels, which only refer to correct gaits.

But if you look at the directive ideas on a test sheet, you will find the requirement of straightness mentioned from Training Level on. While considered more as a desirable feature in the lower levels, straightness becomes an absolute requirement once you move up to Third and Fourth levels. In Fourth Level 3 you find it in almost 16 out of 22 movements in addition to such movements where straightness is an inherent factor. It is further

Calm, forward, straight!

Alexis l'Hotte,
Officier de Cavalerie, 1863

Ride your horse forward and keep it straight.

Gustav Steinbrecht,
Gymnasium of the Horse, 1884

tested as an integral part of the horse's training in such requirements as the rein back, and the canter depart from the walk. These immediately show the judge if correct basic schooling has been done or if the horse has simply been rushed through the various gaits without paying any attention to this absolutely essential principle. Obviously, if not present, each movement is scored lower and will reflect on all three collective marks, as well as on the correct use of the aids by the rider.

The requirement of straightness was recognized by all good teachers of the nineteenth and early twentieth century such as Seeger, Steinbrecht, Seunig, Podhasky, Müseler and others. We must recognize that the symmetrical movements of our present-day dressage simply cannot be executed properly to both sides unless the horse is absolutely straight and equally supple to both sides.

What are the basic conditions of straightness?

• Equal suppleness to both sides, allowing the horse with equal ease to maintain any position from a bending to the

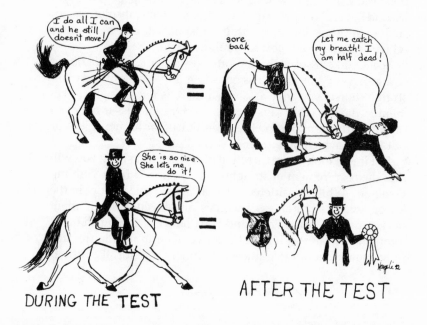

DURING THE TEST

AFTER THE TEST

left to a bending to the right. This is basically conditioned by the freedom of both shoulders.

- Traveling as narrowly as possible behind, which means supporting the center of gravity of the horse and rider as effectively as possible. This is the position that allows for a true engagement, with impulsion and transitions coming from behind. Going wide behind is always a serious fault in itself, and hampers the basic qualities of the true dressage gaits such as engagement, impulsion, self-carriage, and collection.

- Straightness is not limited only to equal freedom of the shoulder. The other consideration in developing a straight horse is that you must obtain equal impulsion and work from both hindlegs. This is so important that many experts consider this just as essential as the freedom of the shoulder. They point out that in a young and untrained horse, one hindleg always works less, shifting the work to the other side. If this is not corrected early on in a progressive way, it becomes accentuated through the years and the one-sidedness, instead of disappearing, becomes more visible. This goal of equal strengths of supporting and pushing power in the hindlegs can be achieved by the same type of exercises as those used for the general suppling of the horse: shoulder-in, shoulder-out, haunches-in, haunches-out, bending, counterbending on a circle in the trot and canter, and countercanter. These exercises will greatly strengthen and continuously develop the power of the hindlegs, as well as ability of balance of the horse in all gaits. Only once a horse is properly trained in this way

The fact is that every horse has an instinctive tendency for a particular kind of asymmetry. If the rider pays no attention to it during the first schooling session (which is almost always the case), the horse settles down in this asymmetry. It organizes, in a way, "its own" asymmetrical form of resistance. ...Since it is unnatural for a horse to remain straight, its straightness must be acquired, or taught, and can only result from schooling, thanks to which its personal reactions will no longer be manifested and its reactions to the actions of the rider will be symmetrical.

Colonel Jean Saint-Fort Paillard,
Understanding Equitation, 1974

will you be able to ride with equal ease to both sides all the movements of the upper level tests.

Anatomy of a Crooked Horse

The following thoughts are intended to help you think through the problem your horse presents, but are certainly not the only ways to look at it. Not every horse is equally crooked or equally deficient on one side than the other. Training must be individualized, and you and your instructor should have a clear concept of what you want to do with your own horse.

If we look at a one-sided horse from above, we see the following:

- The inside shoulder is less mobile but carries more weight.
- The long muscles along the spine are contracted and shorter on the insider than on the outside.
- The long muscles on the outside of the spine are longer, suppler and stretched.
- The inside haunches go under the horse better and are more muscled since they always carry more weight.
- The outside haunches carry less weight, are less muscled, and not as strong as the inside.
- The outside shoulder, which carries less weight, is more supple and freer in its movement.
- The spine itself is basically straight, with the bend shown by angulation of the sacroiliac joint and the unequal position of the shoulders.

Looking at the kinetics of the horse's muscular anatomy, the shoulders are one of the most complex systems of the movement of the horse. The shoulders and front legs have no bony connection to the rest of the skeleton such as the haunches have through the hip bones, the pelvis and the sacroiliac joint. In the shoulders, there is no clavicle to support or fix the front limbs to the sternum as it is the case in humans. In addition, more than 50 percent of the total weight is carried in a muscular and ligamental sling in which rests the chest and rib cage of the horse. Incorporated into this structure are the muscles that makes the front legs move, such as shoulder and pectoral muscles. Then comes the longitudinal muscles and ligaments, which follow the spine of the horse from the neck to the tail, and the attachment of the neck to the withers and shoulders, which must remain in this position. To this arrangements comes the attachment of the long abdominal muscles that affect the movement and engagement of the hindleg. On top of all this, we have the rider and tack adding even more weight to this entire structure.

Therefore, the objectives of our gymnastics are to make all the systems work and integrate smoothly, so that both shoulders can not only slide forward and backward but also move laterally. They should reach around towards the front of the chest equally well with different lengths of stride, say, depending if you are riding a circle or not. Ideally, they do this equally well to both sides.

Anybody who ever had a "frozen" shoulder after a riding accident remember what the smiling physiotherapist did: pulled your arm practically out of its socket, consoling you with a sweet voice, "Just a little more, it won't hurt."

Don't try to do that to your horse! However, regular massage treatment will help to keep those muscles smooth and tightened while you work on increasing the mobility and strengths of both shoulders by consistent gymnastic exercises. A key gymnastic is the circle; the basic and fundamental exercise for every well-schooled horse starts and finishes with riding circles. This was recognized by the masters of academic equitation to the Spanish Riding School. The circle should be progressively reduced in size and then modified in such a way that it can be ridden in a shoulder-in and a shoulder-out, in haunches-in and haunches-out, and in all three gaits. And, if you are very ambitious, you may even go to the concept of the academic equitation of de la Guérinière, where those figures were not ridden as round circles but as small squares. Ultimately, this will result in an equally supple horse, with equal freedom in the shoulders.

Interestingly, while doing this and particularly while riding shoulder-in, we are beginning to exercise and strengthen also the inside hindleg, asking for more hock action, better flexion and more supportive power. Therefore, these type of exercises are not only good for the shoulders but will progressively increase the strength and supportive action of the haunches. Only with this strengthening will the horse be truly able to collect, stay light and on the bit. We must always remember that collection starts from behind and is not a result of a double bridle, or asking for an artificial frame in front.

Any horse can be ultimately made straight, particularly if the rider pays sufficient attention and makes straightness one of her basic objectives. But what I see in the show ring convinces me that inattention of the rider to this basic requirement is present in 80 percent of all horses that move beyond Second Level.

The easiest way to check this is to see it from behind. Look very carefully at any videos you have of yourself shot from behind. In most instances, the video will show you as well as the saddle shifted slightly to one side and your horse going crooked as a result.

Unfortunately, instead of correcting this basic problem with seat position and exercises, we too often see longer and longer spurs, unsteady, rough, incorrect hands, sharper bits, banging legs, and so on. These will never achieve the necessary development of the shoulders and the haunches. So don't ask more of your horse than you ask of yourself. Start by correcting your seat first and you will find improvement in the horse relatively quickly.

If your horse has a perfectly correct position, is becoming absolutely straight and has no difficulty with the exercises and movements referred to above, then you will find the requirement of any test for lateral movements, straightness on the centerline, circles, and other movements in the tests above Second Level very easy, and you will be able to ride fluidly forward, and without any visible aids.

You may ask, why this emphasis on straightness? Why is straightness so important in modern dressage riding? Just watch carefully at any show and you'll soon see the problems that arise when straightness is missing. This becomes more and more evident as the levels advance. Horses will do movements and transitions well to one side and demonstrate evasion and faulty performance to the other. Look at it this way: how can any horse do well if only 50 percent of all symmetrical movements and transition are correct? How can the rider expect 60 percent or more? Let's look at some examples of deficiency in straightness.

The Centerline

How often do you see a truly straight horse on the centerline, with the haunches exactly behind the front legs and the head not bent to one side, keeping his straightness throughout the transitions of the halt and change of gait? Very rarely. Most often, neither the part from **A** to **X**, the halt and transition, or the part

from **X** to **G** are straight, particularly when collected canter is required from **A** to **X**. The same unbalanced crookedness is also evident in the last movement or whenever a movement encompasses a straight section on the centerline.

Obviously, 7's or 8's are not in the cards, and just practicing riding centerlines will not help. The lack of equal suppleness and lack of straightness need exercises to correct, not just doing the same movement over and over.

The Turn at C followed by Medium or Extended Trot

If your horse is still less supple to the right, your medium trot from **M** to **K** will also not be very good. This is because your horse will not turn well, bend, engage and stay balanced in order to give you a good transition with impulsion and engagement at **M**. You will get only a lengthening of the trot, and not a correct medium trot, with a relatively low score as a result. On the other hand, four movements later when you are asked to perform a medium or extended trot from **H** to **F** (the left side), you may get a 7 or an 8. This is a dead giveaway to the judge and you (hopefully), that your horse has the potential, but was never confirmed in basic straightness and suppleness.

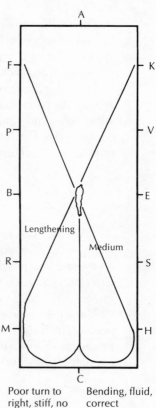

Poor turn to right, stiff, no engagement, no transition

Bending, fluid, correct transition

Circles

In a horse that is not straight and equally supple, trot and canter circles are not shown identically to each side. This defect becomes glaringly apparent in 8-meter figure eights. In fact, correct 8-meter circles to both left and right are the exception, with scores rarely exceeding 4, 5 or maybe a 6, instead of 7's or 8's.

The Shoulder-In and Travers

Judges frequently see a lovely fluid shoulder-in to one side, and an unsteady one that is close to a leg-yielding with a crossing of the hindlegs and a tilted head carriage to the other side. If a half pass is required from the shoulder-in, it will be easy to one side, with a smooth transition but a poor performance to the other side.

These differences become even more evident in the haunches-in and absolutely blatant when you are required to ride a shoulder-in or a renvers on the centerline from **X** to **G**. So whenever your scores show consistent differences between left and right for the same movement, the judge and the test you ride are telling you something very fundamental. You lack equal suppleness and straightness. Go back, correct it now and don't compromise the future of your horse by just pushing ahead anyway and teaching him evasions and incorrect movement to one side.

The Half Pass

What was said for the shoulder-in applies to all lateral work. Any lateral work that is stiff, irregular, or short to one side always reflects a lack of freedom in the outside shoulder. De la Guérinière advised that when your half pass to the left does not go well, go back to the shoulder-in right.

The unequalness will always cut your score to below 60 percent, including collective marks, and if too pronounced will result in an "insufficient," such as in the trot zigzag or the counter changes of hand.

Medium or Extended Gaits and Down Transitions

Engagement, straightness and narrowness behind, while stepping under the center of gravity, is a basic requirement for the necessary impulsion to ride a properly forward down transition. A horse that is not straight and balanced under himself will never be able to do it correctly. Even worse, how is a horse supposed to execute a down transition from behind when the haunches are literally beside the mass of the horse? All he can do is simply barrel ahead or fall on the forehand. Again, in order to ride a correct down transition from a medium and extended gait, the horse must be straight under himself for that transition to come from behind, while remaining light in front, and allowing for an immediate flying change or whatever is required. Since the quality of the down transition is a key factor in judging the movement, the consequences of any lack of straightness are only too obvious in the scores if more evident to one side than to the other.

Advanced FEI Movements

By now you might be bored with this chapter but, like it or not, the truth in riding is often just as unpleasant as in other fields of endeavor. Unequal flying changes with swaying haunches one side, an irregular piaffe with the haunches going more to one side and a crossing of the legs in front with unequal steps, a passage with lack of correct rhythm and cadence with haunches escaping and unequal strides in front or back, pirouettes nice to one side but stiff and above the bit and not bending to the other —all are the result of the deficiency of straightness.

Honestly, how does anybody expect to ride better than 50 to 55 percent from Third Level up on a horse that is not straight, equally supple in the shoulders and willing to step under behind toward the center of gravity with equal power and supporting strengths? Responding equally well to the aids on both sides is only possible if the horse is straight and if the rider truly sits in the middle. If you push your horse beyond First or Second Level before you have been able to teach him these basic concepts or learn them yourself, you risk the chances of your horse ever becoming an upper level horse of good quality, capable of moving higher and higher in the levels.

A Word About Precision

Once your horse is straight and equally supple, and once you know where and how to sit in relation to the center of gravity, and your aids are correct, soft and effective, there is no longer any excuse not to ride with precision. If you ask any foreign judge what is lacking in competitive dressage on this side of the Atlantic, they will all tell you it is a complete disregard of precision and correct transitions at all levels from Training to Grand Prix. I do think things are improving; at least some riders at all levels are beginning to make an honest effort. They probably realize that this is one area, where without too much effort and a little strategy in showing, a significant number of points can be added to their score. The earlier you start riding with precision in the lower levels, the more it becomes second nature as you move up.

While most judges are rather lenient at Training Level, they all expect progressively more when moving up to First and Second levels. But from then on, precision in movements and transitions is just as fundamental a requirement as straightness, and becomes an integral part of the score.

The single most important factor in riding with precision is correct transitions. And correct transitions are based on straightness and the horse's ability to engage behind, and move under himself and do what must be done at a given point under any circumstances.

This precision starts on the first centerline but if you watch closely, how many entries and finishes are really on the centerline? How many halts are ridden with a clean transition at **X**?

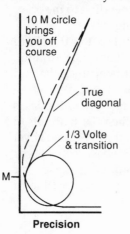

Precision

What we see mostly is halts petering out through the walk or trot and stopping anywhere except at **X**, irrespective of what level we are judging.

How can the rider expect good marks on the extended or medium trots on the diagonal if the horse cannot push himself out of the corner, show the required gaits when finishing the turn at **M**, and be truly on the diagonal and not three or four strides down the long side? Let's not forget the movement *starts* at **M** or **H** or **K** or **F**. So don't blame the judges for not appreciating your superb medium or extended gaits if right in front of him or her, you do not ride an accurate transition and hit the true diagonal.

Let's take a closer look at this problem and understand the inherent difficulty.

First, in analyzing a test it becomes instantly clear that riding straight after the corner makes this turn much easier and an 8 or 10 meter quarter circle is good enough in the lower levels to put you well on the track at **M** or **H**, which is 6 meters from the corner.

But, if you have a diagonal to ride, this won't work anymore and you must ride almost a half volte and a deep corner to finish on the correct line of the diagonal. If this is combined with a transition to the medium or extended gaits, you can only ride it on a truly straight horse who is equally supple to both sides. It is difficult, no doubt.

Unfortunately, what we see so frequently is much too wide a turn, starting the diagonal off course, and showing the transition several strides down the track.

Consider also the trot or canter counter changes of hand that are supposed to go to the quarterline, but usually do not on one side. Or the symmetrical placement of flying changes on the diagonal, or the exact placement of pirouettes. These movements and so many others often point out the lack of precision and, frankly, represent a sloppiness on the part of the rider; it's certainly not the horse's problem!

We will discuss individual movements in a later chapter, so I won't go into detail here on how to ride them with the element of precision. But the point is that once you understand the test and consider this issue of precision, you will find that precision is an added difficulty but also the opportunity for a significant increase in your scores. This makes certainly worthwhile to strive for and develop your techniques to get it done correctly every time you ride.

6:
The Movements

The purpose of this chapter is not to provide "recipes" for each and every movement contained in upper level tests. Rather, my goal to highlight those movements where I most frequently see fundamental problems—and real chances for improvement.

My true goal in this long chapter is to help the reader think through the problems and find their own solutions. By looking at certain individual movements in a thorough way, it is my hope that you will be able to apply this analytical approach to all areas where you find difficulty. It is a *pattern* of thinking that is the lesson here, not the memorization of a prescription.

Circles and Voltes
Riding Corners and Circles

In the strictest sense, riding a corner is simply riding one quarter of a 6-meter circle; hence, its inclusion here. As we move up, riding corners becomes more and more important. Judges look at corners carefully as they reveal very clearly the correct-

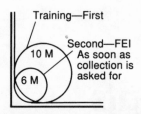

ness and thoroughness of the horse's basic training. As with circles and voltes, judges expect the horse to move through the corner with correct freedom of the shoulders, engaged hindquarters, properly bent in the neck, and on one track. There should be no falling out of the haunches or drifting over the shoulder. Even de la Guérinière considered the corner as a dead giveaway of the sophistication of the rider and the training of the horse.

To understand these movements, let's examine the mechanics by which your horse negotiates a circle or a turn. The ability to flex or bend the spine is a visual illustration and has served the equestrian language very well. It is not surprising that the old masters equated the ability to ride turns and voltes with the degree of freedom and mobility of the shoulders, and the strength of the inside hindquarters to step under the center of gravity and support the greater amount of weight than the other three legs. Interestingly, the old masters do not emphasize lateral flexibility of the spine, which is actually rather questionable.

The diameter of a circle or a turn a horse can do correctly is determined by the freedom of the shoulders to move not only forward and backward, but also around the chest on the outside and back towards the rib cage on the inside. This allows for a lateral direction and different lengths of stride of the two front legs.

Due to the mobility of the sacroiliac joint connecting the pelvis to the spine, this is not such a problem for the haunches when the inside hindleg steps forward and under, and the outside stays slightly back, taking a longer stride on the outside. But the lateral mobility of the spine from the withers to the pelvis is limited by its anatomical structure and even further restricted by the rib cage, the saddle, and the muscular tone of the back and shoulders. These not only have to coordinate the gait, but also swing up and down and carry the weight of the rider.

Taking this into consideration, a horse can look like he is bent around the rider's inside leg, while in reality the spine is relatively straight from the withers to the tail. Perhaps the best illustrations of this are the photographs in Harry Boldt's fascinating book *Das Dressur Pferd*, published in Germany but available in this country.

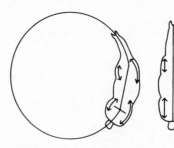

These show the same horse on a circle or a shoulder-in from the front and then photographed from above. In effect, the horse moves like a trolley car around a bend, where the flexible four wheels in the front and back rotate but the trolley car itself stays straight. The difference is that the horse has a flexible neck, which we position according to the diameter of the circle. From this, it should be obvious that the greater the freedom of the shoulder to glide forward and around the chest, the smaller circle we can ride. A young horse whose shoulders only move forward and back cannot do much more than a 20-meter circle as asked for in the Training levels. A trained horse, even a big 17 hand European warmblood, who has truly free shoulders can easily ride a small circle of 8-meters or less without any significant bend in his dorsal spine, even at the age of 20 or more, irrespective of the actual stiffness and arthritis he might have in the spinal column.

Keeping this in mind, we have therefore a progression of smaller and smaller circles in the dressage tests as we move up in addition to the judge's expectation that you ride better and better corners. In light of this, it is clear that the best way to start a circle is not from a straight horse but from a slight shoulder-in or shoulder-fore position, where the outside leg is already moving in the direction of the circle. The horse

... Not only would it be useless to ride through the corners in [this] two-track movement at the present stage of training, but it would actually wipe out any collection we had achieved, for it would relieve the load on the hind legs, which cover a longer distance. That is why the corner is handled as a quarter volte, as is often seen in the Spanish Riding School, the horse's forehand being allowed to reach almost the opposite wall in the shoulder-in. After that it is ridden through the corner on a single track, its longitudinal flexion being maintained.
Waldemar Seunig,
Horsemanship, 1956

The Big Circus

Inside track,
2 horse lengths
Correct volte
for 300 years.

6m

.3m

1921 FEI – 6m
1991 FEI – 6, 8, or 10m
Take your pick!

Magician
Entry fee to performance – $25.00

"The Miracle of the Round Square"

Norquli '92

must stay very solidly on the outside rein which is against his neck. This is actually the deciding factor for how large the circle will be, combined with the support of the inside leg. Pulling on the inside rein has the effect of pushing the horse over the outside shoulder, which ruins any correct circle right from the beginning.

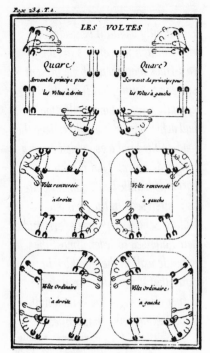

LES VOLTES

from Ecole de Cavalerie, de la Guérinière, 1729.

The Volte

As we look at the concept of the volte, the smallest circle the horse can ride, we see that in the academic equitation of the past this circle was ridden on one track, where the radius was to equal the length of the horse performing it. When the volte is ridden on two tracks, it is the pirouette. In those days, the volte was not limited to a fixed 3-meter radius, but instead by the size of the horse. Since the size of the horse of those days was usually between 15 and 16 hands, this was a reasonable proposition and usually fit within the 6-meter diameter volte of today.

However, with the use today of much larger horses, this concept is slightly in doubt. A volte ridden by the 15.2 hand Connemara Seldom Seen or by the enormous

European warmblood Gifted of 17.2 hands and arbitrary fixed at a radius of three meters is obviously not the same for each horse. This fact of adjusting the volte to the size of the horse was recognized and commented on in the teachings of the sixteenth, seventeenth and eighteenth centuries.

The *FEI Rulebook* states that the volte has a 6, 8, or 10 meter diameter and, if larger, is designated as a circle of a certain diameter. But the FEI as we know it has existed only since 1921. One of the best discussions of the volte is offered by de la Guérinière, on the teaching of la Broue, who lived approximately one hundred years earlier.

Just to show you nothing is fixed in dressage riding, let's look at the definition of what *volte* means over the last 400 years:

- The academic volte was a square, two-times the length of the horse, to be ridden in one or two track position.
- From 1921 to 1991, the FEI defined the volte:

  "The Volte is a circle of 6 meters diameter." (1987 FEI Rulebook)
- From 1991, it is:

  "The Volte is a circle of 6, 8 or 10 meters diameter." (FEI Rulebook 1991)

De la Guérinière's description was then used as a basis by Seeger, Steinbrecht and other authors of the nineteenth century. All indicated the size of the smallest circle a horse can ride is determined by the size of the horse. De la Guérinière stated that the round volte was useful only for cavalry training for actual combat and ridden only to the right in order to get behind the adversary. The volte of academic equitation was a square to be ridden on one or two tracks in all three gaits. The dimensions of the square volte were based on the size of the horse, with the individual sides suggested to be two horse lengths under ideal circumstances. This original concept of the volte has unfortunately been lost today, but if you try to ride it for yourself, you realize immediately that a much greater demand is made of horse and rider. However, the square volte results in a more athletic, supple horse, with correct self-carriage and collection, with flexible haunches capable of progressing to the correct lateral work without difficulty such as pirouettes, passage and piaffe. It is likely that this movement, arbitrary fixed at 6-meters, does not really suit our present-day horses.

It was for very good reason that five years ago the FEI eliminated all voltes from the tests, to the relief of riders, horses, and judges. If you take a look, you will find there are none in the

1991 FEI level tests, from Prix St. George to Grand Prix.

However, there is a volte requirement in the current Fifth Level tests, as in Fifth Level 1:

F - X   Half pass left

X   Volte left 6m

X - G   Shoulder-in left

What are we to do? Obviously, since it is in the test, we must ride it one way or another unless we decide to simply skip it, take a zero and ride happily forward from the half pass to the shoulder-in.

Now, the basic quality of gait we are looking for at this level is forward, rhythmic, balanced and with impulsion, while maintaining the same tempo, bend and position throughout the half pass and shoulder-in as well as the volte. If your horse can ride a correct volte while maintaining all those qualities, you are obviously ahead of the game. But if not, let's consider the options.

Assuming that you must slow down for the volte because the bend is just too much for your 17 hand horse to be able to stay on one track, you will have to struggle to remain on a 6-meter diameter. Your volte, instead of being round, is anything but. To make a smooth transition from the volte to a steady shoulder-in is most improbable. So, you not only get a poor score for the volte, but you also ruin any chance for a good mark for the next movement which in itself should be relatively easy.

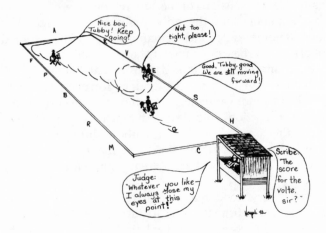

So what are your options?

- Slow down for the half pass. Don't let your horse go freely and rhythmically so you have a chance of performing the volte but at a reduced and slow gait. Obviously, out of this approach, a good shoulder-in is unlikely.

- Ride forward in the half pass, put on the brakes at **X**, crank the horse around, and forego your chance of a good transition into the shoulder-in.

- Ride a good half pass followed by a circle your horse can easily handle, even around 8-meters or a little more, in the same forward quality of gait with balance, rhythm and impulsion with a safe transition to a shoulder-in, showing exactly the same qualities.

It would seem to me that the last option is the best approach. Since you will get an insufficient score for going larger than 6-meters in the volte anyway, a little more or less doesn't really matter, and you will keep your horse happy, going forward, balanced and out of trouble. In this way, you sacrifice a volte for good marks at the half pass and the shoulder-in. Your test sheet should read as follows:

F - X	Half pass left,	*7 or 8*	
X	Volte left 6m,	*4*	Total: 18 to 20 points
X - G	Shoulder-in left	*7 or 8*	

In the first option, your score will hardly exceed 5 or a maximum of 6 for any of the movements; either the shoulder-in or the volte may be insufficient (or both).

The second option offers little difference as to the end results. Your half pass at least should be good. From then on, it is sheer luck or bad luck.

The best solution is to be conscious where your points are coming from and don't worry about it too much. Your co-competitors have to face all the same problems. In this movement, like in so many others, it is often better to sacrifice one movement while trying to do well in all the other ones instead of having a difficulty interrupt the test and actually interfere with one or two movements before or after the problem.

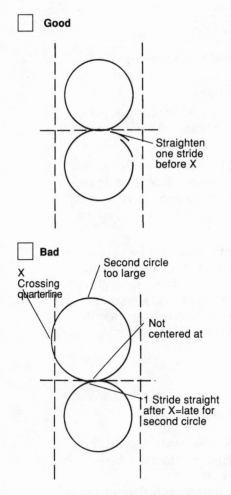

☐ **Good**

~ Straighten
one stride
before X

☐ **Bad**

X
Crossing
quarterline

Second circle
too large

Not
centered at

1 Stride straight
after X=late for
second circle

The Figure Eight

The 8-meter figure eight, ridden in collected trot, in the 1987 Intermediate 1 test was probably one of the most difficult movements in the entire test. Judges only rarely saw it executed correctly.

Now we find 8-meter figure eights as early as Second Level 3, and also in Fourth Level 3, ridden in collected trot. This is a difficult proposition at best.

Riding an individual 8-meter circle is one thing, but to link two together, with the instantaneous transition within one stride, changing the bend and balance while maintaining the rhythm, impulsion, and self-carriage is a totally different matter.

If you want to see just how tight this is (as well as practice the movement), get yourself six ground poles and make two 8-meter squares at **X**. Leave an opening on the line from **E** to **B**. You'll probably be shocked and find that what you thought was a nice 8-meter figure eight is actually far from it. The movement is much tighter than you ever imagined.

However, realizing our shortcomings is the beginning of doing them right. So let's look at the basic requirements, what must be there for a good score.

- Regularity of rhythm. What usually happens is that the horse slows down after the turn at **X**, losing impulsion and rhythm. The bigger the horse the bigger the problem in maintaining this quality.

- Equal bend to both sides. A horse that is not straight does not have a chance in this movement. In addition, with the loss of bend usually one is no longer on the proper track. There is drifting out to the left or right, and the second 8-meter circle is obviously gone.

- A steady rhythm throughout. The temptation is usually to ride into the movement too fast. You cannot ride fast. Here you must be very careful and not ride faster and more forward than you can handle an 8-meter circle to the stiffer side of the horse. It is better to be a little conservative and slow, instead of barrelling into the movement and missing the first transition as well as the second circle. It does not help to put on the brakes once you approach the circles, or when you begin the second circle at **X**. Also, it helps to ride your turn at **E** a bit wide, rhythmically, engaged and balanced. This is more important than a fancy swirl around at **E** since you will need all the balance you can spare once you start the movement.

- Be very aware that both circles have to be equal, 8-meters to the left and 8-meters to the right, with no deviation. The judge at **C** has a perfect angle vision with the quarterlines, from which you have to stay at least one meter. Precision is certainly one of the important points of this movement.

- The movement must be centered at **X**. It is not permissible to begin one circle at **X** and the other one stride further down on the line from **E** to **B**.

- The transition at **X**. We all can ride 8-meter circles by now in walk, trot and canter, so why not this miserable figure eight? In most situations the problem is not the circle but the transition and the requirements that both circles must be correct and anchored at **X**. The judge at **C** can see elements of this movement very clearly.

If one circle is inside the quarterline and the other is not, the circumference is obviously not an 8-meter circle and not centered at **X**. Also perfectly visible from **C** is the regularity of the rhythm for both circles, the degree of bending and the steadiness and equalness of engagement to both sides. What can not be seen is if the rider is really on the line from **E** to **B** or if the horse is really straight at **X**, before bending to the new side. The judge cannot see if the rider cuts a diagonal course, thereby reducing or avoiding the difficulty of the correct transition to the second circle. The longitudinal axis of the circle is also hard to assess.

The judge at **E** and **B** has the best assessment of the movement;

that is usually the judge with the lower score. The movement is executed right in front of this judge, there is no doubt where the quarterlines are, or where the point 4-meters towards **X** from **L** or **I** is. Furthermore, sitting on the line from **E** to **B** gives impeccable vision.

This judge can clearly see if the turn at **E** is really finishing on the line, and if the first as well as the second circle are finished on the line from **E** to **B**, and at **X** or not. They also can't miss seeing transitions from left to right, the horse is correctly straight on the line from **E** to **B**, or if the rider crosses diagonally or bends the horse unequally to the left and to the right. This judge will have no question about the regularity of the rhythm and the aids.

Now let's look hard at the problems here; what are they really?

If we return exactly to **X** from the first circle, ride for one stride straight, make the transition and then start the second circle, we are already 1.2 meters after **X**. This brings our second circle either over the quarterline, which is wrong, or we throw the horse around like a polo pony to stay inside the 2.6 meters which are left for a correct 8-meter circle. The second circle is off-balance, uneven, and with a loss of rhythm and self-carriage. The entire movement where we should see rhythm, bend, and balance is lost. It is almost impossible to overlook these defects when judging at **E** or **B**.

Probably by now you begin to see the solution yourself: compromising a little precision on the first circle by finishing slightly before **X**. This can be done by giving just a little more inside leg in the last quarter of the circle, almost leg-yielding to the line from **E** to **B**, a stride before **X**. This allows for a smooth transition directly over **X**, to the second circle and not one stride later, which will always get you into trouble.

All you have to do is to concentrate on riding the transition and change of direction ahead of your horse, by shifting your weight, and looking to the new side. You have the horse follow you instead of trying to push him into the new direction.

One can only wonder if whoever included this movement has ever ridden a correct figure eight, at least recently and on a horse that is moving up to Second or Fourth Level. Realizing that this kind of exercise may be very good for polo ponies but not dressage horses, the FEI has eliminated it from the 1991 Intermediate 1 test as counterproductive and not in the interest of correct dressage training's objectives.

The Shoulder-In

Not only is the shoulder-in a movement that has to be shown from Second Level on to the FEI Tests, it is one of the most fundamental exercises for dressage. Without shoulder-in, it would be impossible to achieve the degree of suppleness, balance, freedom of the shoulders, engagement, and flexion of the haunches demanded in present-day competitive dressage.

It was de la Guérinière who, based on the failure and frustration of Newcastle, developed the shoulder-in. It was based on his very sound understanding of the kinetics of the horse.

Newcastle had attempted to achieve suppleness and balance by asking for a leg-yielding, either on a circle or on a straight line, but admitted that all he got from his work was a horse that went on the forehand. Many even injured their hindlegs. Newcastle's mistake was that he never took the horse's center of gravity into consideration. He erroneously assumed that simply moving laterally would be sufficient as long as the horse crossed over behind and in front and responded to his aids.

De la Guérinière's intention and impulse in the shoulder-in was that since the center of gravity in the horse is normally not directly supported but instead suspended between four corners, it was important to move support as much as possible directly under the center of gravity. Balance and lightness in front would result, as well as engagement, flexion and strength in the haunches. The lessened weight on the front legs would allowed for more suppleness.

De la Guérinière realized that it was very difficult to make a young horse engage his haunches on a straight line, stepping

Riders most frequently make the mistake of leaning towards the inside. Amongst other inconveniences, this loads the legs which are under the greatest strain. This may be avoided by leaning on the outside stirrup.

Beware of the so-called shoulder-in, so frequently seen, in which the rider pulls on the inside rein while leaning on the same side, with his leg drawn back to jab the horse with the spur, which forces the poor animal to move laterally while remaining twisted, and which takes all impulsion away from the horse, leading to resistance against the rider. ...

The weight should be on the outside buttock as the outside leg acts softly but firmly.

Nuno Oliveira, *Classical Principles of the Art of Training Horses,* 1983

Once the lateral position has been gained, we begin to move laterally, with a leading outside rein. The increased action of the inner leg and inner rein not only maintains the bend, but induces the lateral movement of the horse. The outside and inside leg together control and guide the haunches, and support the outer rein to collect the horse.

Since in this movement the inside leg bends and drives forward, it is logical that the horse reacts to this strong influence by trying to escape the bending by falling out with the haunches. Therefore, it is essential to counterbalance correctly the effect of the inside leg with the outside rein and leg if the gait is to remain rhythmic and correct, and not deteriorate into a lateral falling out.

The rider must often use the outside leg and rein more forcefully in the shoulder-in, and put more weight on the outside, in order to control the outside consistently. This determines the degree or extent of the outside leg's lateral movement as it determines the free, correct, and unrestricted movement of the inside legs.

The control of the outside is conditioned by the collection as well as the increased weight on the

under and toward the center of gravity and carrying more weight. His absolutely wonderful solution was to move the center of gravity over the inside hindleg by moving the front of the horse off the track, while keeping the hindlegs moving straight forward.

By doing this there is more weight placed on the inside hindleg while the front are allowed to carry less and become freer. The basic problem is to avoid having the horse escape this request by falling out with the haunches and finishing in a leg-yielding, a fairly useless exercise, in my opinion. The aids as suggested by de la Guérinière are to bring the front of the horse in by applying the outside rein towards the withers of the horse, while keeping a light inside leg on the girth in the rhythm of the inside hindleg. The weight of the rider should be to the outside since the horse always follows the weight of the rider. In addition, it was important not to put even more weight on the inside hindleg which had to carry the largest part anyway, by sitting to the inside. An outside leg positioned slightly back keeps the outside hindleg from falling out.

It was de la Guérinière's contention that the degree of difficulty and demand on the horse should be progressively increased. While starting with a 30 degree angle, he suggested a progression in the trained horse to 45 degrees, as we see the shoulder-in executed in the Spanish Riding School today.

Podhajsky seriously questions if

a 30 degree shoulder-in really gives us the total benefit we could obtain. It does seem to make very little sense to ask the same 30 degree angle of a Second Level horse as of a made FEI competitor.

In dressage today, the shoulder-in is assessed and judged in accordance with the level of collection a horse is capable of at his stage of training. As you move up to Third, Fourth, Fifth and the FEI levels, judges expect more: more collection, correct seat, quiet hands, no obvious leg aids, the horse moving in an absolute steady rhythm, in self-carriage without tilting the head, and with no crossing of the legs behind.

There seem to be two schools of thought as to the correct aids, particularly the seat and the distribution of weight to the inside or to the outside, when teaching a horse a correct shoulder-in. Putting more weight in the outside seat and stirrup as de la Guérinière indicated, is nothing more than to apply the basic principle that the horse always follows the weight of the rider. This also permits better control of the outside hindleg and prevents the potential falling out of the hindquarters which lead to a leg-yielding.

outside hindleg, which in so doing limits its freedom. The general rule, therefore, is that the outside aids should be predominant while learning these lesson, as long as the outside haunches are not yet flexed, in order to make it progressively more supple by putting more weight on it. Once this improves, the aids become progressively equal until in the made horse the shoulder-in has no visible aids except for the outside rein, controlling the bend and position of the forehand, and the soft contact with the inside leg, maintaining the rhythm and the lateral movement.

Gustav Steinbrecht
The Gymnasium of the Horse, 1884
Translated by the Author

Sitting to the inside is directly opposite to this basic principle of dressage and I have never found a logical explanation why an exception must be made in shoulder-in even though you find it in many books. To me, when you sit to the inside you give the horse contradictory aids. Your weight tells him to move off the track, whereas your leg and spur have to be much more forceful in order to keep him on the track, thereby eliminating any elegance and very often kicking the haunches out into a leg-yielding.

Once the horse is fully trained and confirmed in his movement, the aids can become more and more subtle; just the weight on the outside seatbone is all that's needed.

Nowadays there are different opinions as to the degree of the angle which the horse forms to the wall in the shoulder-in. In opposition to de la Guérinière's theory it is maintained that the forehand should be taken in to such a degree that the inside hind leg follows exactly in the track of the outside foreleg, thus making a single track, so that three instead of four hoofprints appear.This interpretation generally leads to a sort of outline of a shoulder-in, and the inside foreleg does not cross sufficiently over the outside one. In this case the purpose of the exercise—the bending of the three joints of the hind legs, the freer movements of the shoulders, the improvement of the contact with the bit, and the increase suppleness and obedience—will not be achieved.

Alois Podhajsky
Complete Training of Horse and Rider,
1967

The correctness or deficiencies of a shoulder-in are especially evident if it must be done on a centerline from **X** towards the judge. What we frequently see is an over-positioning and leg-yielding of the horse, or nothing more than a twisted neck, with the horse drifting off the centerline. If you cannot do the shoulder-in correctly on the long side, you will obviously have trouble on the centerline. Once, however, you are absolutely secure in your execution of the shoulder-in, it really doesn't matter where you do it. You can do it just as well on the centerline as on the long side.

When you are doing it on the centerline, you must keep the horse's haunches on the centerline, the front legs slightly off. A good way for the rider to realize where she is on the centerline is to be sure the rider's leading knee is always pointing exactly to the letter **C**. This almost guarantees that you are steady on the centerline and absolutely correctly positioned. On such a balanced horse it is very easy to make a required turn correctly once you reach G and to be perfectly prepared for whatever movement comes next.

The Half Pass

The half pass is a movement too often poorly executed in Third and Fourth levels, and even later on at Prix St. George. If not learned correctly from the beginning, it will always handicap your scores. If you look at the tests, you will find that the half pass is one of the key movements from Third Level to Grand Prix, scored both directions.

The half pass should be a logical progression once the horse has mastered shoulder-in, travers and renvers. It is asked for at Third Level from the centerline back to the long side, or from the corner towards **X** or **G**, or **E** and **B**. Other half pass requirements start from a shoulder-in or an 8-meter circle. In the advanced levels the half pass must go clear from **F** to **E** or **M** to **B** with a transition and then back to the other side.

But whatever the test designers ask, every half pass consists of three basic elements: the transition into the half pass, the half pass itself, including the degree of the angle, and then the transition out of it to the next movement. In judging, all three elements are considered for the score by the judge. However, we must realize that if the first transition is missed or is not done correctly, it is almost impossible to recover to a sufficient score and the entire movement is ruined.

What are the features of a good half pass?

- A smooth, forward approach that positions the horse exactly as needed for the half pass.

- The first lateral step with the leading inside front leg should be energetic.

- An absolutely steady bend in the direction of the movement, held from the first to the last step, with no tilting of the head.

- No change in rhythm and no irregular steps in front. The horse should remain on the aids and not fall on the fore-

Each time the horse wants to lead with his hindquarters instead of his shoulders, it is the action of the outside rein in the direction of the half pass which sends the shoulders more sideways. Each time that the hindquarters do not move actively enough sideways, it is the opening of the outside rein in the opposite direction of the half pass which corrects that tendency. The inside rein remains tranquil and through the association of the leg on the same side in the region of the girth, maintains the bend.

Another exercise on our progression; from the centre line half pass towards the wall on reaching the wall, slow down the shoulders and make the hindquarters walk in the direction of the half pass. The Old Classical Masters used to call this "affermir l'appuyer" (to confirm the half pass). The horse stays with the hindquarters close to the wall to half pass along the long side. The bend remains the same and the exercise become the classical exercise named "renverse". When the horse will do this easily down the long side, continue on the short side. In the corner support the shoulders and make the horse walk more on his

Continued on page 76

Continued from page 75

hindlegs so that the horse keeps the same angle. On reaching the start of the other long side begin to ask the exercise of lengthening stride, on the diagonal. The horse will have good impulsion from the renvers and will give good lengthening of stride.

Nuno Oliveira,
Classical Principles of the Art of Training Horses, 1983

hand.

• A correctly positioned rider and unobtrusive aids.

• Finishing the half pass at the designated spot and only then straightening the horse after one stride on the track.

However, how does reality look?

• The horse coming out of a turn or circle being pushed over his shoulder with the haunches leading and too much weight on the leading foreleg. Compounding this sad picture are irregular steps in front and a tilted head carriage.

• A progressive loss of bend with overactive hands of the rider, worsening the situation further until the half pass finishes as a leg-yielding.

• Sloppy riding such as not finishing at the letter, either too soon or considerably after it.

• Incorrect aids and position of the rider such as leaning to the

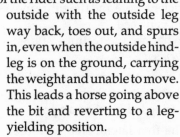

outside with the outside leg way back, toes out, and spurs in, even when the outside hindleg is on the ground, carrying the weight and unable to move. This leads a horse going above the bit and reverting to a leg-yielding position.

• Unequal performance of the half pass to the left and to the right. The horse is not equally supple, responsive to the aids, and not truly straight.

"The Poor Half Pass"

What does it take to ride a correct fluid, half pass with as little effort as possible? First, it is the correct use of the rider's weight. The slightest placement of the center of gravity to the inside is the most elegant and fundamental aid, compelling the horse to move laterally, to catch up with his own equilibrium. Initially, this might have to be a little bit exaggerated, but once the horse has learned, this is a most significant aid. It takes very little effort and obviates any other excessive interferences.

Think about it: how can a horse move freely and elegantly to the left in a half pass with the rider hanging over to the outside on the right? And, if the horse is not truly equally supple and muscled up on both sides, the rider usually sits on the hollow side of the horse irrespective to which side the horse moves. This leads to a good half pass in one direction and a poor one in the other where the use of spurs, whip, and rein aids makes the situation even worse.

If there is any doubt about your position, have a friend take a video from behind and check if you, your saddle, and your position on the horse is exactly as it should be or if, unconsciously, you are always sitting a little bit more to one side.

Besides the change of weight to the inside, the outside leg is an important aid. It induces the outside hindleg and the inside front leg to step laterally. This is possible only when both legs are off the ground and swinging forward. Once they have touched the ground again, carrying 1500 pounds of horse and rider, no force—weight, spurs, whips or kicks—can possibly make them move. The only result will be to make the horse upset. The aids of the outside leg must therefore be coordinated in the rhythm of the hindleg, when the diagonal (outside hind, inside front) legs are off the ground and moving forward. The rider's outside leg should remain inactive and waiting until the diagonal legs are again off the ground. In this way, the ability to respond makes the horse more capable and willing to answer even modest leg pressure. It also assures the rider of

> *While constantly correcting the seat, the instructor should not overlook the rider's legs. There is no great problem when the leg aids are not being applied, but when they are, the rider will be inclined to raise his heels as he may feel that the horse will be pushed forward better in this way. This would, in fact, weaken the pushing aid. The raised heel of the outside leg behind the girth would make it lose its effect and encourage the rider's seat to slip to this side, a common fault often seen in the half pass.*
>
> **Alois Podhajsky,**
> *Complete Training of Horse and Rider,*
> 1967

a quiet and elegant leg and seat, which will reflect not only in the marks for the movement, but in the collective score on the effectiveness and sophistication of the aids. The inside leg at the girth is just as important as it maintains the rhythm and the forward impulsion.

Constant banging of unsteady legs and even the digging in of outside spurs into the poor animal serves no purpose and are counterproductive, particularly when using the heels and spurs further and further back. This leads to the progressive avoidance of the pain on the part of the horse, loss of the bend, and ultimately nothing more but a crooked leg-yielding. This is particularly disturbing to the judge (in addition to the horse) if equestrian prowess, knowledge, and leg position do not match the aggressive and astounding size of the spurs used by many riders. Usually the size of the spur is in reverse proportion to the ability of the rider!

Leg aids are combined with the outside rein if corrections are needed in the angle or the position of the horse in the half pass. If the haunches are leading either from the transition into the movement or while actually riding it, your outside leg should move closer to the girth rather than behind it, so that your heels or spur is not pushing the haunches ahead of the front. You can combine this leg aid with a little more neck reining with the outside rein in the same rhythm as your outside leg. By all means, no spurs or whip and a little bit less inside leg!

You may also use your inside leg to hold the haunches; instead of having your inside leg positioned at the girth, just take it back a little to hold the haunches out. But be careful to not interfere with the rhythm, impulsion and self-carriage.

In an actual test situation, any correction made will be too late. The judge has already seen it and the score will be insufficient. So concentrate on regrouping all the positive elements you have in the horse to be ready with a good transition into the next movement, instead of trying to salvage something that's beyond repair.

If your horse's haunches are falling back, it is most often because your outside leg is not properly coordinated with rhythm of the outside hindleg. Your aids are being applied at a time when the horse cannot respond. This can be easily corrected if you are conscious which of the legs of the horse is moving at any given moment. Sometimes, however, it looks like the front of the horse, at least to one side, has enormous crossing ability, greatly exceeding those of the hindleg. In this case, the rider's inside leg should go forward, holding the action in combination with half halts from the outside rein, allowing the rear to catch up.

Remember the proper role of the hands. How many of us actually have quiet, supportive hands? Our first reaction when something goes wrong, is to push, pull, half halt and move our hands left, right, up and down, further back, or even worse, hang on the inside rein. Then we expect the horse to return to a nice steady position on the bit after having yanked him all around. How absurd! Especially with a younger horse, it is essential that he has a steady, reliable, supportive bit on which he can lean a little when needed or just stay with it for the whole half pass. For most of us amateur riders, the best solution is to take our hands out of the movement completely, while at the same time provide stable support for the horse's head and carriage in the position we want.

How can we do it? The best way I know is to make a bridge between both reins with a shorter inside rein, put both reins into one solid grip of the inside hand, keep both hands together, and leave them on the horse's wither. This position fixes the horse's bend for as long as you want. Since both hands are touching each other, they cannot move around. This works perfectly well in a snaffle but even better in a double bridle where the slightly positioned curb bit leaves the horse no choice but to accept the same bend throughout the movement. Since most of the half passes up to Prix St. George start from a corner, you form the

bridge while riding your approach. Fix the bend for the duration of the movement, then use your other aids such as weight, seat and leg in order to get the movement itself. You then cannot interfere in the position of the horse once he had started to do what you want. Mistakes, poor half passes, and so on can mostly be attributed to poor, overactive hands. Remember, many outstanding teachers, past and present, considered unsteady hands the graveyard of any decent half pass.

The degree of bend in the half pass often causes confusion. By now, an equally supple horse should have no problem in achieving any degree of bend. The only question is what is correct or what does the judge consider correct. If we go back to the 1930's, 40's, 50's and even 60's, we see pictures of horses practically straight with only a flexion at the poll as the exemplary demonstration how to ride the movement.

In those days, the main concern was not to overload the leading front leg, allowing it to move freely and elegantly, This is not possible when the total weight of the neck and head rests on this leg. Positioning the horse, in contrast to real bending, was considered the proper answer to the problem. Later in the 1970's and 80's, more and more bending was asked for, possibly based on the exceptional performance of one horse, namely Granat, ridden by Christine Stuckelberger, whose stupendous lateral ability was always presented in a very excessive bend. This was despite the FEI definition which has not changed.

So what should you do in present-day competition? My own feeling on this is that you should work at home with the old concept of a limited bend and correct flexion at the poll while insisting on absolute regularity of the rhythm, equal strides in front, lightness, uncompromising consistency of position to the end of the movement, and correct unobtrusive aids. When you ride a test in competition, play it more safely. Bend your horse more by shortening the inside rein further when you make your bridge, use the correct weight and leg aids, and let the judge marvel at your performance.

The pendulum of what is correct is still swinging forth and back. It makes no sense to argue with standards of judging at any given moment as long as you understand the fundamentals of the problem and train accordingly at home, adjusting when showing to what is acceptable or required at any given moment.

If you struggle with unequal half passes, you have missed out on the correct basic training. What should you do? Since the conception of the shoulder-in and correct lateral work by de la Guérinière, it has been advocated by all knowledgeable authors that you must go back to the shoulder-in to the other side, until both shoulder-ins are correct and equally fluid and in self-carriage in a correct bend and angle. You will then develop sufficient freedom of the outside shoulder, and your half pass to the difficult side will become just as easy as the one to the good side. Let me just quote what de la Guérinière has to say on this subject. "In a faulty half pass left, the right shoulder cannot reach forward and around the chest. Therefore, the shoulder-in right forces the horse to do exactly that, is a good basic training, and will achieve progressively better and better suppleness leading to the good half pass."

The transition into the half pass from the centerline and back to the long side is the easiest and simplest way to ride a half pass in any test. It is basically nothing more but the repetition of the exercise that taught the horse the half pass in the first place. What ruins the approach and transition into this movement most often is the anticipation of the rider for what is coming and a too early application of the outside aids and shift of weight to the inside. It is not the horse's fault if the horse begins falling in halfway through the turn and start the half pass with the haunches leading, resulting in a score of 4 or less. Therefore, if you are a relaxed rider on an experienced horse, ride the turn as you would to simply aim for the centerline. Once at **D**, from a slight shoulder-fore position, start your half pass. This looks

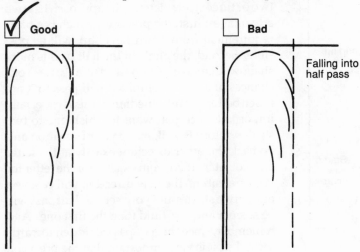

☑ **Good**　　　　　　　　☐ **Bad**

Falling into
half pass

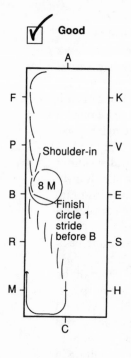

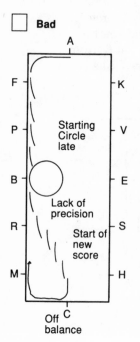

elegant, easy and uncomplicated. But if you are just starting out with a young horse and are yourself not sure or skilled enough to ride a correct half pass or to correct the position of the horse if faulty, try the following approach. Ride the corner with the techniques advocated by de la Guérinière where, after the corner, you bring in the front of the horse with your outside rein, while keeping your weight slightly to the outside. In this position, ride through the half turn and finish on the centerline in a slight shoulder-fore position. Only then apply your outside leg and shift your weight to the inside, after having made the bridge I mentioned earlier, between the shorter inside rein and the outside rein. From then on, by having the horse following you and using your outside leg in the rhythm of the outside hindleg with the inside leg maintaining the impulsion, you should have no problem riding your half pass to **B** or **R** or wherever you want to go.

A half pass from the corner to the centerline is actually easier since your turn is limited by the ring. Ride it in the shoulder-fore as recommended by de la Guérinière, but go deeper into the corner so you can start at the letter and not two or three strides later. This approach has two advantages: first, the precision which is a basic requirement from Third Level up, will be possible. Second, the angle of the half pass is more shallow than when you start too late. Your chances of a fluid, not forced half pass to **X** are much better. At Intermèdiare II this is especially important since you want to finish one to two strides before **E** or **B**, make your transition and go back the other direction exactly at the letter and not later. If you aim exactly for the letter for your transition, the new direction will cost you one or two strides and your second half pass will be steeper and less fluid than the first one. And remember, since the half pass is ridden towards the judge, it is very important that the precision and the transition to the other bend is smooth and supple. You don't want to force the issue during the last few strides.

The transition to half pass from a circle such as in the Prix St. George test should be relatively easy provided, you plan ahead properly. The 8-meter circle at **E** or **B** from a shoulder-in is easy but, since the horse is leaning in with more weight on the inside front leg, you must put him back into a vertical balance. This takes the weight off the inside front to some extent so the first stride laterally can be free, dramatic and light. This can be done by asking for one stride in shoulder-fore before applying the aids for the half pass.

When judging, what I see most often is that this transition is done too late, losing one or two strides on the track before starting the half pass. This results in a rather steep half pass with a chance of losing the impulsion, and finishing well after **G**. If this is the case, your turn from the centerline to **H** and **M** will the be off balance with no chance to get a correct transition to a medium or extended trot as stipulated. The mistakes that ruin this movement were made back at **E** or **B**, in the circle to half pass transition.

The worst that I see is the rider throwing the horse over the inside shoulder when coming out of the circle, stumbling towards the centerline with irregular steps in front, a loss of bend, unsteady position and a desperate uncoordinated rein interference by the rider who attempts to save what is not salvageable.

Therefore, if you have trouble it might be safer to take the following approach. Start your circle one stride before **E** or **B**. This is only a minor imprecision and hardly noticeable from **C** and **M**. Then, ride a correct circle but start a shoulder-fore position one stride before **E** or **B**. You will then be ready by **E** for the half pass on a completely balanced horse. You won't have any difficulty reaching the centerline slightly before **G**, giving you one stride in order to straighten out, rebalance, shift your aids for a correct turn. You can then have a powerful transition forward into a dramatic medium or extended trot. The key to a good half pass and then a good medium or extended trot depends to a very large degree on the execution of your circle and the transition out of it. Much too frequently I see riders riding a correct circle and then taking two or three strides on the track before starting the half pass, which becomes too steep for the ability of the horse to execute nicely.

The transition from shoulder-in to half pass should be an easy

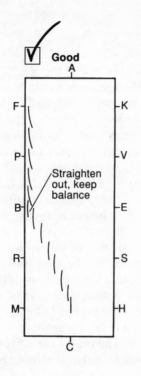

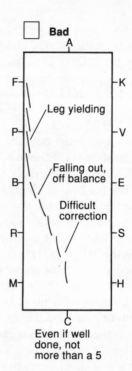

Even if well
done, not
more than a 5

one, particularly if the shoulder-in is executed correctly and not exaggerated. The rider's aids should be properly shifted from the outside seat and inside leg to an inside seat and outside leg at the time of the transition from shoulder-in to half pass. This does not require any rein action and the position bend of the shoulder-in is the same as for the half pass.

However, some of the problems which you see all the time are totally predictable if you carefully observe the shoulder-in or what should be a shoulder-in. If the rider's inside leg is too far

back, and if one of the humongous spurs usually used is continually pushed into the ribs of the horse, the haunches will fall out. Instead of a correct shoulder-in, we see a sort of a leg-yielding with the hindleg crossing from the inside to the outside, resulting in a loss of engagement and self-carriage. Making a correct transition from behind into a half pass from this situation is impossible since the horse is not engaged. The outside hindleg would either hit the inside when asked to cross or, more often, the horse just takes one straight step forward before responding behind while the front of the horse is already moving laterally. This leads to the loss of the haunches, which fall out.

When the haunches fall out, self-carriage and engagement are lost, the horse is on his forehand and the resulting half pass is insufficient. So, if this happens to you, don't worry about the half pass: correct the shoulder-in which is the basic flaw in your performance.

Since in competition we are often tense, this can happen to all of us while doing the shoulder-in but why ruin the next movement too? A safe way, irrespective of what happened before, is to bring the front to a shoulder-fore position and keep the bend. After having done that, ride your transition as described earlier into the half pass.

The Canter Half Pass

The same principles apply for the canter half pass as for the trot half pass. However, in the trot work we are perfecting shoulder-in, travers, renvers, straight lines and circles, having the horse properly prepared for the half pass. So these movements are required in the proceeding competitive levels, but this is not true for the canter half pass.

Looking at many canter half passes, I sometimes get the feeling that few of the horses has ever been properly prepared to be comfortable in the lateral movement. Most finish on the forehand and ruin the transition that follows.

If you follow the teaching and training recommendations of riders from de la Guérinière up to our time, you find that some exercises applied to the trot are also applied to the canter. Many riders work forever in shoulder-in, travers, renvers at the trot but once they start work in the canter, all they do is canter around and around on a crooked horse. Shoulder-in, travers, and renvers are just as (if not more) important done in the canter in order to teach the horse balance, consistent engagement, collection, equal suppleness and straightness. If done early and consistently in training with transitions into the canter from the walk, halt and rein back, a canter half pass is a piece of cake when required at Third Level. You must realize that it is important to teach the horse the same basic movements in the walk, trot and canter. The easiest way to ride a transition into the canter half pass without having the haunches fall in when riding the turn is to apply the aids and have the horse understand. Ride a few strides of shoulder-in, from which the transition into the canter half pass by just shifting your weight is relatively easy. Then the horse's haunches are neither leading or falling back, and the horse is balanced on his inside hindleg for the entire duration of the movement.

There is a very good academic exercise for the half pass: alternating shoulder-in to half pass to shoulder-in and so on, both in the trot and canter. This makes the horse wonderfully supple and confident in your aids. Also, since horses in early training have the tendency to go a bit more on the forehand and less engaged behind, the shoulder-in serves as a collecting exercise. This puts the horse back on his haunches and reestablishes collection.

Canter Work
The Canter Entry

While in the lower levels the entry is done in trot, beginning at Third Level you must enter at the canter. All of the considerations I outlined in **The Competitive Edge** for the lower levels are just as valid here. However, in the canter entry you have an additional consideration over the entry in trot. While the trot is a symmetrical gait—left diagonal, right diagonal, left diagonal, right diagonal—and therefore consistently supports the center of gravity, this is not true in the canter. In the canter you always move on one diagonal only, moving from the right or left hindleg into the left or right front leg. There is still debate today at the FEI Levels over whether the horse in canter can be really and truly straight, or there is always a slight or minimal position which would be accepted as correct. The minimum that we expect to see is that even with a slight bend the hindlegs follow exactly in the track of the front legs.

Looking at 99 percent of horses in a canter entry, there is no doubt but that they are a little bent, even when traveling on a straight line. Most of them have a tendency to let the inside haunches fall in a little bit which immediately affects the quality of the transition to the halt at **X**.

While I recommended in **The Competitive Edge** that in the trot you enter on the inside of **A**, I recommend here that if your horse is not yet absolutely straight in the canter, you enter from

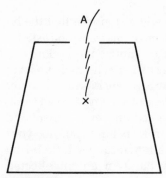

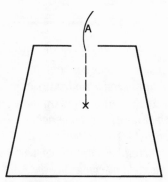

Inside of A
- Greater possibility of haunches falling in
- Poor control for the transition to the halt as haunches are not under horse

Outside of A
- Soft turn to left onto centerline after A
- Keep shoulder-fore position
- Haunches following on one track
- Good transition from engaged hindquarters at X

the outside of **A**. This allows you to come back onto the centerline, and think "shoulder-fore" in the canter down to **X**. It assures that the haunches don't fall in and are correctly positioned under the horse for a good transition from an engaged inside hindleg to a good halt. Out of this halt, it is not too difficult to make a straight, forward transition into the trot without any walk steps. If you know the exact number of canter strides you need to get from **A** to **X**, usually more or less 12, a score of 8 should be the rule for you and not the exception.

As in the trot, using shoulder-in in the canter is an excellent exercise to develop suppleness, engagement, balance and self-carriage. For the rider, it helps develop the feeling of really controlling the haunches. It is also the beginning of teaching the horse a balanced countercanter, and one of the best exercises for developing a collected, engaged gait with the horse fully in self-carriage and round and steady in front of the rider's legs.

The Canter Depart

Starting with Second Level, except Second Level 3, all canter departs are either from the walk, the halt or the rein back. Only in Intermediate 2, Grand Prix and the Grand Prix Special is transition done from the proceeding passage. This makes it very clear that this transition must already be the training program while riding First Level.

The way in which the strike off at the canter should be done has been the object of innumerable controversies.

The Comte d'Aure provoked the strike off at the canter to the right by using his left leg, after having slightly turned the horse's hindquarters to the right by employing the left rein.

Baucher, in his first method, used diagonal aids. His example was followed by James Fillis, and by nearly all the écuyers of that time. But at the end of his career, Baucher finished by using interior lateral aids.

Each one of these ways is good. The most essential thing is to give the horse the appropriate gymnastic preparation in order to strike off in the canter by pre-determined aids.

The horse must be well impulsioned, and well cadenced at a canter in three beats time, and he must hold himself straight on each hand, (this is the most difficult thing for a horse) before he starts to flying changes or pirouettes.

One of the most beneficial exercises for obtaining flexibility, straightness, and unification of the forehand with the hindquarters, is the shoulder-in at the canter, along the side of the wall.

Nuno Oliveira,
Reflections on Equestrian Art, 1976

You will also notice that the introduction of this transition asks for a collected canter, and no longer a working canter. This makes a lot of sense since a transition to the canter from the trot always starts in front, with no need for engagement and thrust from behind, putting your horse automatically a little bit on the forehand in an uncollected frame, which is very difficult to convert to a collected engaged canter once established. On the other hand, cantering from the walk forces the horse to push off from behind with better engaged haunches, giving automatically the correct frame and power of the collected canter and making it much easier to continue as required. In order to avoid this effort, the horse has a tendency to use one or two strides of trot, thereby defeating the purpose to go into a collected canter and finishing on the forehand, which obviously results in an insufficient score for the transition and a loss of points for the ensuing canter movement.

What we are looking for in the transition is straightness, a transition with thrust from behind, the horse light on the bit and forward, and a complete first canter stride, not just a hop.

What do we often see? The haunches falling in, lack of engagement and impulsion, not forward or up, transition through trot steps, leaning on the bit and going on the forehand.

The key to this canter depart are aids that allows the horse to do it:

namely a slight shoulder-fore position, engaging the inside hindleg, primarily inside aids and legs and allowing the first canter stride by releasing the inside rein and keeping the outside rein steady.

These aids have been consistently advocated by the old masters as well as modern riders such as Steinbrecht, Heidelbrecht, Seunig, Podhajsky, Storl, Oliviera, de Nemethy, Boldt, the German Riding Federation, Decarpentry, and so on. However, unfortunately, we very often do not see the rider follow these good examples.

Teaching the horse early the canter from the walk is an excellent preparation for correct flying changes as the horse learns to associate the aids with pushing through from behind and not just responding in front and following behind later.

The most difficult canter depart and an unforgiving test for correct schooling and throughness if properly executed is the canter depart from a rein back whereby the horse must first make a square closed halt, back four strides, straight, effortless and collected, followed without hesitation by a collected forward canter while remaining absolutely straight, collected, light and on the bit. This movement only used up to now in FEI tests has been incorporated in a difficult sequence of movements in Third Level where neither horse nor rider are ready for it in most circumstances.

The Canter Serpentine

C - X	Serpentine in 2 loops, width of arena, no change of lead
X	Circle left 10m
X	Simple change of lead
X	Circle right 10m
X - A	Serpentine of 2 loops, width of arena

What a movement this is, found in Third Level 1 and 1-S. It certainly takes all the skill you can muster at this level. Even with a more advanced horse, it is often nothing but problems because there is never a break to reorganize. Furthermore, it is rated by five separate scores out of a total of eight canter scores in the test. Even at Prix St. George, the horse is given a break of 12-meters after the countercanter to the flying change and then another 12-meters approximately four strides before the next countercanter. So if you want to ride this movement and this test, at least be aware of what you are getting into and never blame your horse if it does not work.

The fundamental requirement to succeed is to have a horse that can stay truly collected and balanced and can hold a slight shoulder-in in the countercanter. Approaching the first serpentine of 30-meters, ride a bit conservatively, crossing the centerline three meters before going into the countercanter at **I**. Then, try to get on the line from **B** to **E** a little early in order to have a good one and a half strides before **X** so you can rebalance your horse, begin the 10-meter circle at **X** and, hopefully, stay within the two quarterlines. If your countercanter loop finishes at **X**, you will not be able to stay within the quarterline, or start your circle at **X**. You will then be automatically rated insufficient. Also remember, you must be straight on the line from **E** to **B**; crossing diagonally into the figure eight or on the serpentine change of direction is a serious fault. Come back from the first circle as in the trot figure eight, try to move onto the line from **B** to **E** a bit early, and, remember, you *must* be straight, with no diagonal crossing. Furthermore, you must not ride your down transition before you reach **X**; if you do, you are not riding a correct 360 degree circle, which will lead to an "insufficient" performance.

Then the test asks for simple change at **X**. This is in itself impossible since the simple change requires 5 strides more or less: the down transition, three walk steps, and the transition back into the canter. Where does that leave you? If you stay on the line from **B** to **E**, you will be already over the quarterline, and the positioning of your second circle is gone along with an acceptable score. And, if you ride your simple change on the circle track, you will be around a quarter of the circle before you even pick up the canter. But the test states: canter, right lead at **X**, which in this configuration is an absolute impossibility. So you have two options: your second circle is either not centered on **X**, or is only ridden three-quarters of the way in the right lead canter.

Which option you pick is up to you, both being insufficient unless there is someday a general agreement between the judges that this is the time to take a sip of coffee or finish the doughnut. But then how many doughnuts can you eat or cups of coffee can you drink when you have a big class? Discussing this particular movement with a visiting FEI judge from Europe, he commented that a correct canter figure eight can only be ridden with the flying change and even then is very difficult at best. He was unable to understand why this movement was in at Third Level when we should be trying to give our horses confidence, allowing them to move forward without bringing in too difficult a transition and changes of directions all at the same time.

So if you are to come out of this more or less sufficient, you must go back into your countercanter and the canter serpentine in the same way as we discussed for the first part of this long movement.

Now what about in the short arena as in Third Level 1-S? If you squash this movement into the short arena, the canter and countercanter loops are just 10-meters, the same as in Intermediate 1 and Prix St. George. However, here you have no break in which to rebalance and reorganize your horse or regain his collection if he fell a little bit onto his forehand. Therefore, if you ride this test in a short arena, and you do not have a horse of at least Intermediate 1 or 2 training accomplishment level, you will be asking for a lot of problems.

In Fourth Level 1 and 1-S, we have:

A   Collected canter, right lead

A - C   Serpentine in three loops, width of arena, with flying change of lead on crossing the center line

If you are getting 7's and 8's on this movement, don't change anything—you must be doing it correctly! But, if you are getting 5's or 6's or even 4's, with the judge's comments of "late behind," "change not on the centerline," "horse falling over shoulder," "cutting across diagonally, or "half-circles not of equal size," and so on, you may be pretty frustrated by now and somehow at a loss, particularly if your horse does nice changes when set up differently.

Let's break the movement down into its parts:

• Three equal 20-meter half-circles.

• No corners at **H**, **M**, **K** or **F**.

• An absolutely straight line across the centerline in a 90 degree angle.

• The change on the centerline—not before or after.

• Equal bending to both sides and in a steady rhythm, with the horse consistently on the aids.

What does the judge see quite frequently?

- Unequal bending since many horses are not yet equally supple as they should be at Fourth Level.
- Different size half-circles, as a result of the above.
- Crossing diagonally, which avoids the difficulty of the serpentine as well as the flying change.
- Flying changes after crossing the diagonal.
- The horse thrown over the inside shoulder into the new direction and, as a result, changes that are late behind or even crosscantering for a few strides.

Why is there so much trouble in a simple exercise connecting 20-meter half-circles with a flying change?

The basic problem is that at this stage of the horse's training, the flying change must be properly set up. It takes a half halt on the outside, a change of bend to the new lead with the soft inside rein becoming the solid supporting outside rein. Then the old outside rein gives, allowing the change to go through, and the weight and the seat of the rider shift to the new inside. All this must happen in two strides at most.

What faces most riders is that on a 20-meter half-circle, the horse is much more bent than when riding regular flying changes on straight lines or out of a half pass. The change to the new bend must be made more dramatic than as when going straight. What happens is that most riders force the flying change before the horse is really positioned in the new direction and ready for the

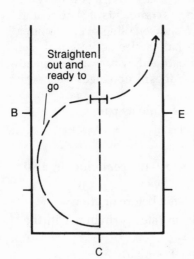

change, thereby disturbing the balance and correct engagement of the new inside hind-leg. Remember, you have only two strides to get ready, one before the centerline and one on the centerline for the flying change itself. But having a well-bent horse coming from the serpentine makes this rather difficult. Therefore, I recommend that in the last part of the half-circle of the serpentine when leaving the track, you straighten the horse so that when you are coming towards the centerline, you are sitting on a straight horse and not one that is still bent to the inside. This makes it easier for the horse, as well as for you, to get a clear forward change, through and from behind, without throwing the horse over the new inside shoulder like a polo pony. The change of aids is not so abrupt and unbalancing. The same type of approach, that is, riding the horse straighter when coming out of the turn from the track, can also be used in the canter—countercanter—canter—serpentine movement in Intermediate 1 where the circles are much tighter and the bend of the horse often greater.

Counter-canter

After Second Level the quality of the counter-canter must be better, and judges expect to see progressive improvement as the levels advance. But we still see the same basic mistakes at the FEI levels as at Second Level. The reason for this, I believe, is that very few riders school their horses in the canter in renvers, travers and shoulder-in as they do in the trot.

The best quality counter-canter is achieved when your horse can handle a shoulder-fore to the outside in a 10-to 15-meter half or full-circle. This will lead you to be exactly on one track, not overbent, no haunches falling out, consistently collected and never in four-beat. But how often do we see that? I would say very rarely, indeed.

So teach your horse shoulder-in and haunches-in in the canter as well as the trot, and try to ride the square volte of de la Guérinière in all gaits. This will develop into a correct counter-canter. It assures you will be on one track, with no four-beat canter, or falling on the forehand. It will also allow for very easy flying or simple changes, as may be required at various stages from Third Level on up.

The counter-canter movement in Prix St. George is a lovely movement when ridden correctly:

R - I   Half-circle of 10m diameter right followed by half-circle

I - S   Left in counter-canter

S - E   Counter-canter

E   Flying change of leg

The counter-canter part of the 10-meter half-circle should be no problem if time has been spent training in the shoulder-in at

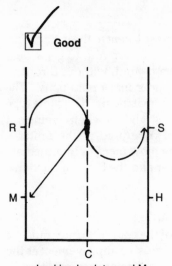

Good

- Looking back toward M
- Shoulder fore
- Counter-canter in
      shoulder fore
- No falling out of
  haunches

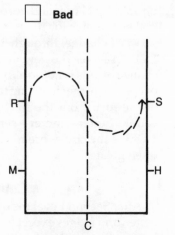

Bad

- Looking straight at judge
  and C
- Haunches still on
  circle
- Crossing diagonally, -2
  points!
- Haunches likely to fall
  out in counter-canter

the canter. Why then do so many rides not score more than 5's and often even less? Here are the most frequent mistakes I see:

- The first half-circle is less than 10-meters, avoiding the difficulty of the counter-canter. This varies from 11-to 12-meters in diameter.
- The rider crosses diagonally, never riding a real 10-meter half-circle, again avoiding the difficulty of the movement.
- Drifting out in the counter-canter onto two tracks.
- The horse overflexed, his haunches falling out in a four-beat canter and on the forehand.

These mistakes are all a lack of precision, frequently from over anticipation of the counter-canter. It is better to concentrate on positioning the horse correctly for the counter-canter—and then let him do it. By now, the horse should know exactly what is expected from him. The counter-canter is, furthermore, toward the enclosure of the ring so let him do it—he won't jump out! Ride him forward and don't throw him off with your hands, legs, spurs and other interfering aid which make it much more difficult for the horse to perform well. Be even a little softer with your hands and let him balance himself during the movement to maintain his self-carriage and the necessary forwardness. Even if he does go a little bit on the forehand, this is better than going into a four-beat canter, throwing out his haunches and losing impulsion and falling over the shoulder.

The one part where you absolutely must ride correctly is the transition from canter to counter-canter on the centerline, right in front of the judge at **C**. The horse must be straight on one track for at least one stride and exactly on the centerline. Most often what we see are the haunches never lining up with the front and then, as the logical sequence, starting the countercanter on two tracks. The haunches then consistently fall out and the horse crosses diagonally without ever being straight on the centerline. The reason for this is that when we come with a nice bend from the first half-circle, and the front of the horse and the rider face straight towards the judge, the horse's rear end is still on the circle and not properly lined up on the centerline. I always found it best to ride as if I wanted to go back to **M**: look at **M** instead of at **C** and the judge before beginning the counter-canter. I then look to my next point of repair, namely **S**. This assures that you are properly on one track and lined up while keeping the bend on the centerline, and prevents the haunches falling out in counter-canter. Also, from this position it is relatively easy to ride a little bit of shoulder-in in the counter-canter to be sure that you do not lose the haunches. Considering everything as equal, a horse ridden like this will be at least one point up and sometimes even two, whereas crossing diagonally with haunches falling out is a definite lose of one to two points.

The Canter Pirouettes

Riding or teaching a pirouette can best be subdivided into two totally separate problems, if you want to be successful. If either of these problems is not understood or mastered by the horse and rider, the pirouette as a whole will not work. What are they?

1: The ability of the horse to collect and practically canter on the spot, on a straight line, and not on a curve or bent line. This so-called *durchlassigkeit*, to collect, engage and lower the croup on a straight line, is the basis of the movement and must be learned and practiced by itself before even thinking of a pirouette.

2: The riding of the pirouette itself is often best done from a rather wide turn on the haunches in the walk by simply continuing the movement in the canter until the horse understands what is asked of him.

Only once 1 and 2 can be easily done on both leads should a real pirouette be attempted by connecting the two elements together. Also when attempting to correct a faulty pirouette it is absolutely mandatory to understand which of the two elements is the cause to correct it properly.

The first detailed description resembling what we look for in the pirouettes today is in the *Ordini di Cavalcare* (Rules of Riding) by Frederico Grisone of Naples, written in 1552. It was executed in three or four canter strides. At this time, the pirouette was absolutely essential in hand to hand combat on horseback. Since then, the movement has been stylized, discussed and modified and became one of the academic movements of dressage riding.

The *FEI Rulebook* states that pirouettes can be ridden in collected canter, walk or in a piaffe with the inside hindleg as a pivot maintaining the same footfall as the gait in which it is executed. Today, in a full canter pirouette six to eight strides are correct. In judging, it is not only the pirouette itself but the approach and the transition into it that must be evaluated.

Reviewing the literature since Grisone, there is one fact for the canter pirouette to which all authors agree: the importance of the approach. But from that point, the variety of opinions is almost as great as the number of authors writing about it, including the enormous variety of techniques for teaching the horse the pirouette. For us, the most important lesson is the fact that

> *To prevent the horse from falling in to the pirouette, he should be given a slight shoulder-in position before this exercise. At the same time, collection must be well established because, if the horse becomes 'long" before starting the exercise, it will fail.*
>
> **Alois Podhajsky,** *Complete Training of Horse and Rider,* 1967

> *Without careful preparation the aids for the pirouette would come as a surprise to the horse, who would then throw his body into the turn with irregular strides. If horses show this tendency it is mostly to the left and it happens because in preparation the outside hind leg was not brought sufficiently underneath the horse's body. To correct this fault the rider must improve the horses's straightness.*
>
> **German National Equestrian Federation,** *Advanced Techniques of Riding,* 1986

the canter pirouette consists of the further collection of the canter beyond collected canter to an even more compressed canter, almost on the spot; if this is not executed or feasible with a given horse, there will never be a good pirouette. This is because the horse will not be able to become lighter in front, or more engaged and rounder, the position out of which the pirouette must be ridden.

If we consider the types of canter ridden in the academic equitation of the Renaissance and best described by de la Guérinière in *Ecole de Cavalry* and *Elements de Cavalry*, we find first mention of a "school canter." This is probably closest to our present-day collected canter. But going even further on the issue of collection, de la Guérinière defined further types of canter. The first is the *gallopade*. Here is how it is described:

> If a horse has strong joints and has developed very active movement with the haunches, a four-beat canter develops, namely the gallopade. This four-beat is essential for a beautiful gallopade whose primary distinction is the decisive and active stepping under of the haunches that reduces the action of the forehand. The footfall in the gallopade to the right is left hindleg, right hindleg immediately followed afterwards by left front leg and last right front leg.

Taking collection even further we arrive at the *redop*. In the chapter on this gait, de la Guérinière refers specifically to Newcastle, who in his opinion gives the best description of a canter in a two-beat rhythm, almost on the spot, whereby the two hindlegs and the two front legs move together. This is essential to understand since depending on whom we read, we find reference to all three types of canter. Subsequent to the canter we see them referred to in regard to the pirouette and the approach to it.

Another important aspect to consider is that when we analyze the canter with slow motion cinematography, we see that there is no real three-beat canter but only a four-beat, even if we don't see it. But there is a gray area between an obvious four-beat canter and an apparent three-beat canter and judges may honestly disagree. The difference in interpretation is based on the limitation and variation of visual perception which is different from one human being to the other.

This is similar to the great variation in auditory perception where certain individuals can discern almost each individual instrument in a symphony orchestra when others fail to appreciate it and only understand the beat of steel drums. There is also no doubt that the visual and auditory capabilities of animals far exceed those of humans but we have no choice but to live with our individual sensory limitation. It is not surprising that many riders, trainers and judges can discern the rhythm of a four-beat canter by listening to the footfall a long time before they see it and vice versa.

Most of the authors of the eighteenth, nineteenth and early twentieth centuries recommended the highly collected four-beat canter, the gallopade, or even a redop in the last steps before the pirouette. These include Steinbrecht, Oliveira, Seunig and, as mentioned, de la Guérinière. Others simply speak of a highly collected canter without any further reference.

While the ideal number of strides in the pirouette mentioned most frequently is between five and eight, Steinbrecht states that the pirouette in one stride can be ridden from a redop on an outstanding horse and in two strides with a good horse. De la Guérinière does not mention the number of strides which he considers correct and ideal.

There is even some disagreement and questions raised about if the horse truly pirouettes on the inside hindleg. Seunig as well as Wynmalen raise well-founded doubts that this may not always be the case. They indicate that the outside leg can be just as much a pivotal point because that is where the canter stride originates, even though it carries less weight than the inside hindleg which steps under the center of gravity as it moves on a small circle.

What we always see with pirouettes up to Grand Prix is the inability of the horse to really collect from behind on the straight line. Instead, the rider begins the pirouette on a small circle and once the inside hindleg is engaged, finishs off the pirouette with four correct pirouette strides. In order to make this requirement absolutely clear, we are required in the Grand Prix to ride the pirouette on the centerline, straight towards the judge, where any such deviation gets heavily penalized. In working toward this goal, we should ask for engagement of the inside hindleg in a slight shoulder-in position, from which the pirouette can be ridden more easily. Here again, as in so many of the dressage solutions, the answer to the pirouette is not to practice it to exhaustion but to improve the throughness of the canter on a straight line to more collection, proper preparation after which the pirouette itself is relatively easy.

Either at Fourth Level or Prix St. George, the angle, pattern and position of the half pirouette is not so tightly predetermined as later on. It is still a serious mistake, though, to start from the wrong approach. The most difficult pattern is required in the Grand Prix Special where you have not only two pirouettes on the centerline, but where the two pirouettes are connected by 9 tempe changes, which again must be absolutely straight. The strength of the haunches, the balance and the aids of the rider must be absolutely perfectly coordinated and this is certainly one of the most difficult movements to ride correctly.

Flying Changes in Sequence

Beginning at Fourth Level, you are required to perform flying changes in sequence, instead of a single change. There are a number of considerations to take into account to gain a good score on this movement; let's look at some of them.

In practice, one often finds that horses will do better on the changes every three strides instead of every four. Maybe there is more rhythm to every three, or perhaps horses are only able to count to three, feeling that more than that is higher mathematics! If this holds true for your horse, you are certainly better off working on tempe changes every three strides instead of four. Later on, when your horse is sufficiently secure, he will wait for your aids and not assume what you want to do.

The basics must be correct. The horse must be straight, as we have talked about earlier. Any horse whose haunches are swaying to both sides, or to one side only, is lucky to get a 5. Once a horse is at this stage and lacks straightness, it is very difficult to correct. The omission from proper training at the earlier levels begins to take its toll. It has definitely compromised the progression of the horse and, since the horse has learned an evasion consistently, it becomes practically impossible to correct.

The changes should be light and forward. Excessive rein and not allowing the change to come through with a giving new inside rein are the main cause of this defect. We too often see changes getting progressively more labored and more and more on the forehand, flat and shorter. The description from the *FEI Rulebook* makes this very clear:

This change of leg is executed in close connection with the suspension which follows each stride of the canter. Flying changes of leg can also be executed in series, for instance at every 4th, 3rd, 2nd or at every stride. The horse, even in the series, remains light, calm and straight with lively impulsion, maintaining the same rhythm and balance throughout the series concerned. In order not to restrict or restrain the lightness and fluency of the flying changes of leg in series, the degree of collection should be slightly less than otherwise at collected canter.

By this time the horse should understand what is asked of him, and wait for the rider's aids, which should be subtle and unobtrusive. The throwing of the rider's weight from left to right with legs flying forwards and back, will depress the score of the movement as well as collective marks. Most likely, the horse will not be able to keep his balance and go straight and relaxed as we wished. Fundamentally, these are no longer aids but interferences with the horse's balance as he tries his best to stay on four feet. The elegant way you see in the Spanish Riding School and with some advanced riders is quiet, almost silent, leg aids, with simply a slight raising of the shoulder to induce a change.

It is important to place the movement correctly on the diagonal. To earn good scores, the changes must be placed as symmetrically as possible. Too often we see changes finishing after the letter **M** or **H**, or **K** and **F**. The horse is then thrown into the corner simultaneously with the last change. Similarly, we see flying changes rushed before **X** and then the horse cantering on happily for the rest of the diagonal. It is, therefore, essential for every rider moving up to the tests requiring a sequences of changes to understand the basic principles and move beyond the idea that changes just have to be done somewhere, somehow, in order to secure a good score.

Assuming your changes are correct, straight, forward and equal, the movement has an additional dimension—symmetry. The number of canter strides before starting and after finishing the movement should ideally be the same. Here is one way to go about which has very well worked for many riders.

• Count the number of canter strides from **F** to **H** (or any diagonal you want to try). On a big, forward moving horse, even in collected canter, 20 to 22 strides is all you

need. On a smaller horse, cantering with shorter stride, this may go up to 26 to 28. Whatever this number of strides, this is the baseline for your strategy of riding.

- The sequences of changes are always in uneven numbers (3, 5, 7, 9, 11, or 15) in order to finish on the correct lead at the other end.

- In order to satisfy the principle of symmetry, the middle change of the sequence should be made at **X**. For example, if the requirement is three changes, the second change is at **X**. If five changes are required, the third is at **X** and so on. Once you know the number of strides your horse needs for the diagonal, you can calculate the number of strides between the first and last change.

Let's assume your horse has 22 strides on the diagonal, and you must ride five changes at every three strides. This uses 12 canter strides. This leaves you ten strides, five before and five after the movement at **M** and **K**. Therefore, count five strides after the corner, ride your sequence, then finish with five strides before the letter. You should have your third change exactly at **X**. If the quality of your changes is correct, this should easily count for an 8 or even better on your score.

You can even make up your own table as shown below for absolute accuracy, tailored to your horse's strides.

This system, however, does not hold exactly for the single tempe changes since the horse is usually more collected and the canter strides on average are shorter. You may need to add at

Type of changes (changes every stride)	Total Canter Strides on Diagonal	Number of strides within the Movement	Strides before the Movement	Strides After the Movement
3 x 4	22	8	7	7
3 x 3	22	6	8	8
5 x 4	22	16	3	3
5 x 3	22	12	5	5
7 x 3	22	18	2	2
7 x 4	Obviously impossible!!			
5 x 2	22	8	7	7
7 x 2	22	12	5	5
9 x 2	22	16	3	3
15 x 1	22	14	4	4

least one stride or even more at the beginning and the end of the movement but your basic calculation is still the same.

A key consideration is that the fewer strides you have going into the changes, the better your approach must be. Therefore, your corner must be much deeper and ridden on a straighter horse so that when you come out at **F**, **K**, **H**, or **M**, you are already balanced, straight and ready to go whenever you apply the aids for the first time. There is no way you can just coast through the corner and expect a good series of multiple changes.

7:
Understanding the Tests

In the lower levels, analyzing and selecting a test is very important, as we discussed in **The Competitive Edge**. As we move up it becomes even more important to completely understand what the intent behind each test is and to approach them with greater sophistication, level by level.

The ability to analyze an individual test or tests in a given level is the key to competing successfully. Unless you understand what is being asked of you and your horse, and it matches with both of your abilities, you may never really understand the reasons behind the good or bad scores. You will just continue to simply ride a pattern from letter to letter as you did in Training Level and get bad scores.

The first thing to note is that following the sequence of tests within any level is not necessarily the best for you and your horse. And, using the exact same elements, one could design an easy test with no difficulty or an unrideable monstrosity.

The dressage arena in the upper levels is nothing more than a mine field, with booby traps and little devils just waiting to throw you off the right track and into trouble, with nobody inside to help you out of the pickle but yourself. The best solution is to avoid problems. This is possible if you know how, when and where you may run into trouble, and to understand the problems ahead. You can then decide whether to face them or not.

In many clinics I have been asked by riders about one movement or another with which they consistently have trouble. Once explained, they realize either the real difficulty involved or how they should ride them correctly. The general comments I get is, "Gee, I never thought about it this way." But that is exactly what you should do before you decide on any test.

Let's take an analytical look at the Third Level tests to see this illustrated.

In the very first movements, the entry and first turn at **C**, there is already a significant difference among the tests. Test 1 and 3 have a smooth turn and an easy transition to a shoulder-in or a straight section with no problems. Test 2 goes directly into a medium trot on the diagonal from the turn at **C** to the right, which means riding three-quarters of a 6-meter circle in the corner. This should affect the speed you select when moving off from **X** since you not only have to ride a tight turn in the corner to end up truly on the diagonal, but also must ride a solid transition forward into the medium trot. At this level there is no more compromise on quality of gait or precision.

In Third Level 1 and 3, on the other hand, it is only after the half pass from **V** to **I** or **P** to **I** that a medium trot from the corner is required. Since the half pass usually slows down the horse, you are better prepared for the turn and the medium trot. As for the 8-meter trot circles in Third Level 1 and 3, the circles are placed by themselves or ahead of the half pass, making them easier to ride.

But in Third Level 2, we head after the medium trot into a sequence of moves worthy of FEI status:

F - X	Half pass left
X	Circle left 8m
X	Straight ahead
I	Halt, rein back 4 steps, pro-ceed immediately
I	Collected canter left lead
C	Track left

Interestingly, the last part was only seen before in the 1987 Prix St. George test. To ride this forward correctly, and perfectly straight on the centerline is, in my opinion, asking too much of a Third Level horse.

So, the trot requirement and transition to the canter in Test 1 and 3 are not unreasonable, but in Test 2 you need a more advanced horse than this level is supposed to be.

Looking at the tests from the prospective of the trot work, we see immediately that there is no progression of difficulties from Test 1 to Test 3 but is actually the opposite. Furthermore, in Test 1, both medium and extended trots start from a right turn corner, so if your horse is still crooked to the right, lucky you! If he is crooked to the left, you can expect two low scores. The symmetry of the test has not been adhered to and this benefits some riders. In Third Level 2 and 3, though, medium and extended trot alternate in a perfect sequence; they will show any shortcomings of straightness, unequal freedom of the shoulder, or power of the haunches.

Now let's look at the canter work in Third Level 1. There is one movement that really counts:

C - X	Serpentine in 2 loops, width of arena,
	no change of lead
X	Circle left 10m
X	Simple change of lead
X	Circle right 10m
X - A	Serpentine of 2 loops, width of arena,
	no change of lead

This movement counts for five of the eight canter scores in this test. The serpentine loops are 15 meters wide, quite a change from the 20 meter loops required in Second Level. Then, after the countercanter, there is no break as is given even to the horses in Prix St. George in the similar movement. Immediately you are required to execute a 10-meter circle to the left, which is certainly a balancing act in moving from right to left at **X**.

This leads into the simple change at **X**. No simple change can be done exactly at any letter; it takes at least five strides to do it— one down, three walk steps, one up. But here, the second circle after the simple change starts, as defined by the test, also at **X**, an impossibility in itself. The second circle to the left is followed by a countercanter serpentine to **A** of 15 meter loops. When you are asked to squash all this into a 40 meter arena as required in Third S-1, your difficulties are even more difficult.

In comparison, the canter requirements in Third Level 2 are simpler, with the exception of the canter depart from the rein back. You have to ride the same serpentine but without the figure eight at **X** and with only a simple change at **X**. If you have mastered the down transition from the countercanter as asked for in Second Level 4, you should be able to do this one, too.

In Third Level 3, the canter demands are child's play in comparison. There is not one trap, not one circle, not one countercanter. There is a flying change wherever you like it between two letters after the half pass; a good First Level horse will give you that as well as any hunter hack. This particular test doesn't even have any canter circles in it, a definite omission, in my opinion, for a championship test, which is difficult to understand.

So what is the sequence of difficulties at Third Level? Test 3 is the easiest. Test 1 in the short arena is the most difficult. Where do you want to begin? What I would do is show Second Level 4, Third Level 3, Fourth Level 1 and leave out the two in the middle which I do not believe appropriate for Third Level horses.

Now let's look at Fourth Level, not only the test themselves but in relation to Third Level and FEI requirements. The trot work in Fourth Level 1 is exquisitely simple, clean and forward with nothing more asked for than shoulder-in, half pass, or a

The Latest Gossip

centerline with 8-meter circles, halt, rein back and a simple transition into the trot. This is no comparison to Third Level 2, with the half pass leading into a 8-meter circle, a halt, rein back and canter depart. Unfortunately, the ASHA gives us no explanation why the trot work and its transitions at Fourth Level 1 should be so much easier than what is demanded at Third Level.

The only new movement in the trot is a medium trot on the diagonal with 7 to 8 collected steps in the middle over X, a clear test of *durchlassigkeit* and straightness which should be no problem for any horse at this level. If it is, questions should be raised by the rider as to if the horse has been pushed ahead too fast and should go back to more basic training.

In Fourth Level 2, the only thing asked for at the trot that matters is half pass from the corner to X and back to the corner, with no specification of allowing a straight section at X. But, really, by now this should be no problem on a straight and equally supple horse, and the shallow angle of the half pass allows for a fluid forward ridden movement.

Now what about Fourth Level 3? It is basically a copy of the 1987 Intermediate 1 including three counter changes of hand in half pass and a 8-meter figure eight. Both of these movements were eliminated in the 1991 FEI test. Nothing like this is even asked for in Prix St. George or Fifth Level 1. One wonders if the objective is to punish an upcoming Fourth Level horse with such requirements. Fourth Level is supposed to be a preparation for FEI Levels, not a copy of more advanced FEI Tests.

So, in analyzing the trot work we see that the regular trot work of Fourth Level 1 and 2 are less demanding than Third Level work but that there is an enormous jump to what is really FEI level requirements in Fourth Level 3. What is even more amazing is the fact that the 8-meter figure eight has already been asked for in Second Level 2, while in the old tests the first time it showed up was in Intermediate 1. Most of the time then it was poorly executed.

Looking at the canter work, Fourth Level 1 is not any more difficult than Third Level 3. The canter serpentine in three loops is no problem for most horses, provided they are properly positioned early enough. In Fourth Level 2, the only real new thing is a 8-meter circle at C after a half pass and flying change, and a canter diagonal with three flying changes of lead following. If the sequence was reversed, this 8-meter circle would be a major headache. Furthermore, three change every four strides by now are a proper progression to the Prix St. George requirements.

In Fourth Level 3, most canter requirements are leading to or equal to the Prix St. George test such as half-pirouettes, three and four tempe changes, and extended and medium canter. A very good movement is the half pass from **A** to **B** or **E**, a 20 meter half-circle in countercanter with a flying change at the letter **E** or **B**; this is imaginative and rides well. In a way it is similar to the movement in Second Level 4 with a simple change, which even on an FEI horse is more difficult to ride than the flying change at Fourth Level.

Looking at it in an overview, then, Fourth Level 1 is on the whole easier than Third Level 1 and 2, Fourth Level 2 is a fair preparation for Prix St. George and Fourth Level 3 is a mixture of Intermediate 1 and Prix St. George. Depending on your horse and your own experience in riding FEI horses and FEI levels, you may or may not agree with the above assessment. But for serious competitors, it is important that for the rider and the horse that a clear picture of the progression or regression of difficulty is in mind as the entry blank is filled out. The test should be appropriate to the ability of the rider and training of the horse.

A similar approach should be applied for assessing the Fifth Levels as well as the latest FEI tests.

8:
Riding the Actual Test

Now let's apply what has been said in this book as we show Tubby and coach him through Fourth Level Test 3. This is the test that is basically a combination of Intermediate 1 and Prix St. George; we'll ride it together.

Tubby is a big powerful Hannoverian with tremendous gaits and a corresponding rear end. His attitude is that "work is for the peasant" and he should just watch. So, he often requires additional encouragement (and convincing) in his work. He is unflappable, except for raccoons in the indoor arena! We keep all of this in mind as we ride the test.

We see while looking at the arena before our ride that after dragging the ring A is not where it was and the centerline is not exactly in the geometrical center. We must adjust our plan accordingly so as to not fall into this first trap. Riding around the ring before the bell we do transitions, collected to medium and extended trot, which is the first movement after the centerline. Once the bell rings, we quietly finish what we are doing and get ready with our prepared strategy to ride the test.

A	Enter collected canter
X	Halt, salute, proceed collected trot
C	Track right
MXK	Medium trot
K	Collected trot

Since Tubby's right canter is better and therefore has the better transition to the halt, we pick up the canter outside **B** toward **F** and **A**. We are not coming into the ring inside of **A** as we would in the lower levels but instead ride a wide circle approaching **A**, almost straight but outside the letter. While riding the line from **A** to **C**, we try to keep a slight shoulder-fore position, to be sure Tubby's haunches don't fall in and the transition to the halt will be straight and clean.

Since we have 12 canter strides to **X**, all we have to do is count to 10, ride a solid half halt followed by a full halt, and relax while saluting. If we are square, fine; if not, we are at least straight and exactly at **X**.

In the transition from **X** to the collected trot, we use a little vibrating rein to alert Tubby. Then we trot on, allowing and giving a little with both reins so he can use his neck and head to counterbalance the first stride, taking off straight and with a full, long step. Then we ride conservatively in view of what is coming, with soft half halts on the right side, in good rhythm but not too forward. We aim for the inside of **C**, while already beginning to put more weight on the right seatbone. The judge sitting exactly at **C** can only see too well if we are drifting over the centerline to the left while it is very difficult to ascertain how forward we are riding after **X**. But the judge will have a perfect vision of what is coming: the turn at **C** and the transition to the medium trot from **H** to **K**.

Since Tubby's extensions are not the best, riding a bit conservatively beforehand will show a more impressive difference. We then ride the maximum extension he can give to get a good score. The real extended trot comes later in the test so a true comparison is relatively difficult. Also, riding conservatively the turn at **C** with a deep corner at **M** (three-quarters of a 6-meter circle) will put Tubby exactly on the diagonal, and not three strides down the track. Since we start the transition while turning, we should have our first medium trot stride at **M** or, at most one step later. We hope that the precision of the turn and transition will be noticed by the judge and support the score for the not-so-extraordinary medium trot, instead of reducing it. We don't want the comment that's given so often: "Poor transition, not on diagonal."

At **K**, remembering the angle of vision from **C**, we come back to collected trot a bit early, two strides before **K**, using the space gained for the down transition. We do this in view of the problem ahead, and just hope this lack of precision will not cost us too much or anything at all.

A	Down centerline
D - G	Three counter changes of hand in half pass, the first half pass to the left and the last to the right of 4m, the other two of 8m
C	Track right

Since Tubby has a tendency in the canter as well as in the trot zig zag to let his haunches fall in, in anticipation (probably the rider's fault), ruining the score by his haunches leading in the first part, we ride the corner from **K** and turn to the centerline in a shoulder-in to a shoulder-fore position, with our weight in the middle, or slightly in the outside stirrup. Since Tubby was a guinea pig for some of the movements of academic equitation, this method as advocated by de la Guérinière of riding shoulder-in through the corner works very well for him. While riding in shoulder-fore after the corner we make a bridge with the reins, with the left one shorter. When we reach the centerline at **D** we shift our weight to the left and use the right leg in the rhythm of Tubby's outside hindleg. Since the counter change of hand is only 4 meters, we don't even have to go to the quarterline, the location of which is perfectly visible from the position at **C** and very well known to the rider if he has looked at the ring beforehand.

In the transitions of the half pass back and forth, we coordinate our weight changes and rein and leg aids, allowing one straight stride to keep the balance, rhythm and impulsion as needed. We will try to finish one or one and a one half strides before **G**, ride straight for 2 strides and reposition Tubby for the turn at **C**. This is right in front of the judge who is, we hope, thoroughly impressed with our accuracy and technique. This should look a lot better than our falling out of the last half pass into the turn if we finish directly at **G** or later. Maybe the judge will give us an additional point for precision and style, if one of

the legs of the zig zag was itself not good enough to keep the
score up.

B	Turn right
X	Circle right 8m
X	Circle left 8m
E	Turn left

What comes now is obviously the low point of the test, the 8-
meter figure eight at **X**. Tubby, with his rather large rear end, is
not an inspiration to look at from behind while we go down the
long side from **M** to **B**. Each time we ride this test we wonder
what prevented the test designer to ask for a shoulder-in here,
to add some elegance, produce collection and engagement and
thereby helping the rider and horse and the view of the poor
judge! So we do it anyway, riding a little bit of a shoulder-fore,
rhymthic, collectic, and prudent in order not to offend the judge
and giving no reason to complain of not being straight. This
gives us the best collection, lightness and self-carriage Tubby
can muster.

Then we ride a turn of a soft 8 to 10-meter radius onto the line
from **B** to **E** to maintain our rhythm, balance and engagement.
We approach **X** in a shoulder-in position by bringing the front
in and not kicking out his rear end. Then it's on to the first 8-
meter circle, trying to stay well inside the quarterlines, like a dog
with a zap collar avoiding the invisible fence. We keep Tubby
always on a solid outside rein with the outside hand close to the
withers and with equally supporting leg aids. Completing
three-quarters of the circle we ease off a little and then leg yield
a little bit towards the line from **B** to **X**. We change our weight,
change the bend and ride directly over **X** into the new 8-meter
circle. Again, we try very hard to stay inside of this 8-meter line,
and ride the new 8-meter circle to the right as well as we can. By
now Tubby is tense; (he hates this movement, too) his eyes are
rolling around like saucers and his flexion is not soft anymore.
But we are approaching **X** and there is a simple section from **X**
to **E** and back up to **A**. To ease the tension, we scratch his withers
with the right hand which is not visible from **C** after we turn at
E. Then, as a courtesy to the judge, again a little shoulder-fore
up to **K** and around the corner. Since we are so far away from
the judge and have our back to him, we can even tell our big
friend in a low voice that he was good boy and assure him that
what is coming is only half as bad as he thinks it will be.

FXH	Extended trot
H	Collected trot

Here we have the same approach to the extension as we did to the medium trot and again we go absolutely for the maximum, hoping that it will not be too poorly rated by the judge.

C	Halt, rein back 4 steps, proceed collected walk
M	Turn right
Between G & H	Half pirouette right, proceed collected walk
Between G & M	Half pirouette left, proceed collected walk
H	Turn left
S - F	Extended walk
F	Collected walk
	The collected walk

The halt and rein back are no problem, but in the walk pirouette Tubby likes to step out on the first stride, no matter what. So, ready for this, we make the first step like a half pass, which is not correct but safer than risking a step out or, worse, a step back. Also, we carry the whip in our outside hand to make sure Tubby doesn't completely forget where his rear end is.

Since Tubby is very good in collecting the walk, as he has been taught to do the piaffe from the walk, it is very easy to show a dramatic change at S going into the extended walk. We let him really walk forward on as long a frame as possible since there is no problem in getting him back when we ask. The transition at F is not a problem and since we are turning our back to the judge, he really can't see too much of how much of a half halt is taken.

A	Collected canter right lead
KXM	Medium canter
M	Collected canter and flying change of lead
H	Proceed toward X
Between H & X	Half Pirouette left
H	Flying change of lead

M	Proceed toward X
Between	
M & X	Half Pirouette right
M	Flying change of lead

Now we can relax a bit. Tubby's canter work is forward and uncomplicated. He loves flying changes, is never late and always well off the ground. His specialty is changes every two strides with a few tempi changes mixed in, even in the medium canter.

At **A**, we do a nice forward canter depart and a transition to medium canter in the turn without being too concerned about being very precise. But we will try to come out of the corner with as much impulsion as we can muster. The down transition to collected canter at **M** is not demanding, and the flying change is tremendous, clean, forward and off the ground. We ride the transition to collected canter in the corner with a shoulder-fore position with half halts on the short side. Again, we ask for more collection in the corner at **H**, starting on a straight line and trying to maintain this collection. In order to prepare properly, we ride the pirouette after three to four strides and from a shoulder-fore position. Although Tubby takes a small curve in his approach, the rhythm and size of the pirouette are perfectly acceptable.

Out of the half-pirouette, we ride a forward flying change and, again, reestablish collection in both corners for our approach to the right pirouette. This time it succeeds from an absolutely straight line ridden in a slight shoulder-fore position in order to engage the inside hindleg.

| H - K | Extended canter |
| K | Collected canter |

We then maintain a conservative canter on the short side but ask for a dramatic transition to the extended canter at **H**, beginning in the last stride of the corner so that by **H** we are flying with full, long strides down the long side. In order to appear straight, and prevent Tubby's haunches from falling in or a quick change of lead when the down transition comes, we take a slight shoulder-fore position. This helps us to get a good transition and, riding the down transition with half halts on the inside rein, eliminates the possibility of an accidental change at **K**. However, on the down transition we can go a little bit easy since it's in the far corner of the ring and our backs are to the judge. Here, the angle of vision makes the assessment of precision much more difficult. This hopefully will not hurt our score.

A	Down centerline
D - E	Half pass left
E - B	Half circle 20m, no change of lead
B	Flying change of lead
A	Down centerline
D - B	Half pass right
B - E	Half circle 20m, no change of lead
E	Flying change of lead

While riding the turn from **K** to **D**, we make a bridge between the two reins, shortening the left one considerably. Then, assured of a slight shoulder-fore position, before we are at **D** we ask for the half pass that takes us without any change in position down to **E**. A small problem for us always exists in the transition at **E** into the countercanter because in previous tests there was always a flying change at the end of the half pass. To be sure nothing like this happens, we maintain our weight to the outside and don't give an inch on the bridge so there is nothing Tubby can do but to continue in countercanter on an easy 20 meter half-circle. Then we allow the left rein to slide, asking for a little bend to the right, and the flying change at the letter is no problem. It is actually a relief for Tubby and so almost comes by itself. We use exactly the same technique to the new direction.

FXH	Change rein, 3 flying changes of lead every fourth stride
MXK	Change rein, 3 flying changes of lead every third stride

Now we have three changes every four strides and three changes every three strides. We want those changes to be straight, forward, off the ground, and effortless. With Tubby's 22 strides on the diagonal, we know we have six to seven strides to get started, which brings the second change exactly at **X** of our three times four strides series.

But since Tubby only counts up to three, we get him more solidly on the aids, to make sure he waits for the fourth stride. We are not much concerned with collection here but really ride forward.

The same approach goes for the three changes every three

strides except we take eight strides out of corner so our second series of changes is placed as accurately and symmetrically as the first one. The rhythm of this change suits Tubby so much better that we don't worry about any mistakes and can ride forward and relaxed with only minimal aids to indicate the changes.

A Down centerline

X Halt, salute

Our last problem is the centerline. To get this correct, we must go back to collection at **K** and, in order to avoid the haunches falling in, ride the turn in a shoulder-fore. We then continue with a slight shoulder-fore position down the centerline. We know that from **D** to **X** we have ten strides so at the eighth stride we give the first half halt and then at ten, a full halt. Again, even if we are not absolutely square, we are definitely straight and definitely at **X**, with no walk in the transition. Having followed our basic plan, we are rather content with ourselves. We congratulate Tubby with a pat on the neck and walk out of the ring.

Now the big question: what is the score? But, really, at this point, who cares? We had a plan of how to ride and tried our best, preparing ourselves and Tubby as well as we could. So we are certainly both entitled to a little stirrup cup after cooling out and settling down, irrespective if we have done well. If somebody else has won the class, then so much more congratulations to them for having ridden even a little smarter.

And once again, don't forget your horse!

Appendix:
AHSA Tests,
Second Through
Fifth Level

SECOND LEVEL TEST 1

NEW REQUIREMENTS:
Shoulder-in in trot, rein back

INSTRUCTIONS:
All trot work is done sitting

NO.

		TEST	DIRECTIVE IDEAS	POINTS	COEFFICIENT	TOTAL	REMARKS
1.	A X	Enter collected trot Halt, salute, proceed collected trot	Straightness on center line, transitions, quality of halt and trot				
2.	C HXF F	Track left Medium trot Collected trot	Quality of turn at C, straightness, quality of trots, transitions				
3.	E	Circle right 10m	Quality of trot, roundness and size of circle				
4.	E-H	Shoulder-in right	Quality of trot, execution of movement		x2		
5.	MXK K	Medium trot Collected trot	Straightness, quality of trots, transitions				
6.	B	Circle left 10m	Quality of trot, roundness and size of circle				
7.	B-M	Shoulder-in left	Quality of trot, execution of movement		x2		
8.	C	Halt, rein back 3-4 steps, proceed medium walk	Quality of halt and rein back, transitions				
9.	HXF F	Free walk on long rein Medium walk	Straightness, quality of walks, transitions		x2		
10.	A	Collected canter right lead	Calmness and smoothness of depart				
11.	E	Circle right 10m	Quality of canter, roundness and size of circle				
12.	M-F F	Medium canter Collected canter	Straightness, quality of canters, transitions				
13.	KXM	Change rein, at X change of lead through trot	Straightness, calmness and smoothness of transitions				
14.	E	Circle left 10m	Quality of canter, roundness and size of circle				
15.	F-M M	Medium canter Collected canter	Straightness, quality of canters, transitions				
16.	HXF	Change rein, at X collected trot	Straightness, balance during transition				
17.	A X	Down center line Halt, salute	Straightness on center line, quality of transition, trot and halt				

Leave arena at free walk on long rein at A

COLLECTIVE MARKS:

Gaits (freedom and regularity)			2		
Impulsion (desire to move forward, elasticity of the steps, suppleness of the back and engagement of the hind quarters)			2		
Submission (attention and confidence; harmony, lightness and ease of movements; acceptance of the bridle and lightness of the forehand)			2		
Rider's position and seat; correctness and effect of the aids			2		

FURTHER REMARKS:

SUBTOTAL _____

ERRORS (–_____)

TOTAL POINTS _____

SECOND LEVEL TEST 2

NEW REQUIREMENTS:
8m circles in trot, 20m serpentine in canter / counter canter

INSTRUCTIONS:
All trot work is done sitting

NO.

		TEST	DIRECTIVE IDEAS	POINTS	COEFFICIENT	TOTAL	REMARKS
1.	A X	Enter collected trot Halt, salute, proceed collected trot	Straightness on center line, transitions, quality of halt and trot				
2.	C R	Track right Circle right 8m	Quality of turn at C, quality of trot, roundness and size of circle				
3.	B E	Turn right Turn left	Quality of trot, quality of turns				
4.	V	Circle left 8m	Quality of trot, roundness and size of circle				
5.	F-B	Shoulder-in left	Quality of trot, execution of movement				
6.	B-X X-E	Half circle left 10m Half circle right 10m	Quality of trot, roundness and size of half circles				
7.	E-H	Shoulder-in right	Quality of trot, execution of movement				
8.	MXK K	Medium trot Collected trot	Straightness, quality of trots, transitions				
9.	A	Halt, rein back 3-4 steps, proceed medium walk	Quality of halt and rein back, transitions				
10.	FXH H	Free walk on long rein Medium walk	Straightness, quality of walks, transitions		x2		
11.	C	Collected canter right lead	Calmness and smoothness of depart				
12.	C-A	Serpentine in 3 loops, width of arena, no change of lead	Quality of canter and counter canter, execution of figure		x2		
13.	K-H H	Medium canter Collected canter	Straightness, quality of canters, transitions				
14.	MXK	Change rein, at X change of lead through trot	Straightness, calmness and smoothness of transitions				
15.	A-C	Serpentine in 3 loops, width of arena, no change of lead	Quality of canter and counter canter, execution of figure		x2		
16.	H-K K	Medium canter Collected canter	Straightness, quality of canters, transitions				
17.	A FXH H	Collected trot Medium trot Collected trot	Straightness, quality of trots, transitions				
18.	B X G	Turn right Turn right Halt, salute	Quality of trot, straightness on center line, quality of turns, halt, transitions				

Leave arena at free walk on long rein at A

COLLECTIVE MARKS:

Gaits (freedom and regularity)	2	
Impulsion (desire to move forward, elasticity of the steps, suppleness of the back and engagement of the hind quarters)	2	
Submission (attention and confidence; harmony, lightness and ease of movements; acceptance of the bridle and lightness of the forehand)	2	
Rider's position and seat; correctness and effect of the aids	2	

FURTHER REMARKS:

SUBTOTAL _____

ERRORS (–_____)

TOTAL POINTS _____

SECOND LEVEL TEST 3

NEW REQUIREMENTS:
Simple change of lead

INSTRUCTIONS:
All trot work is done sitting

NO.

		TEST	DIRECTIVE IDEAS	POINTS	COEFFICIENT	TOTAL	REMARKS
1.	A X	Enter collected trot Halt, salute, proceed collected trot	Straightness on center line, transitions, quality of halt and trot				
2.	C HXF F	Track left Medium trot Collected trot	Quality of turn at C, straightness, quality of trots, transitions				
3.	K-E	Shoulder-in right	Quality of trot, execution of movement				
4.	E-M M	Medium trot Collected trot	Straightness, quality of trots, transitions				
5.	C	Collected canter left lead	Calmness and smoothness of depart				
6.	E	Circle left 10m	Quality of canter, roundness and size of circle				
7.	E	Simple change of lead	Calmness and smoothness of change		x2		
8.	E-K-F FXH	Proceed in counter canter Change rein, no change of lead	Quality of counter canter and canter, straightness				
9.	M-F F	Medium canter Collected canter	Straightness, quality of canters, transitions				
10.	A V L P	Collected trot Turn right Halt, rein back 3-4 steps, proceed medium walk Turn left	Quality of halt and rein back, transitions				
11.	B-H H	Free walk on long rein Medium walk	Straightness, quality of walks, transitions		x2		
12.	C B X	Collected trot Turn right Circle right 8m	Quality of trot and turn, roundness and size of circle				
13.	X E	Circle left 8m Turn left	Roundness and size of circle, quality of trot and turn				
14.	F-B	Shoulder-in left	Quality of trot, execution of movement				
15.	B-H H	Medium trot Collected trot	Straightness, quality of trot, transitions				
16.	C	Collected canter right lead	Calmness and smoothness of depart				
17.	B	Circle right 10m	Quality of canter, roundness and size of circle				
18.	B	Simple change of lead	Calmness and smoothness of change		x2		
19.	B-F-K KXM	Proceed in counter canter Change rein, no change of lead	Quality of counter canter and canter, straightness				
20.	H-K K	Medium canter Collected canter	Straightness, quality of canters, transitions				
21.	A D X	Down center line Collected trot Halt, salute	Straightness on center line, quality of trot and halt, transitions				

Leave arena at free walk on long rein at A

COLLECTIVE MARKS:

Gaits (freedom and regularity)		2	
Impulsion (desire to move forward, elasticity of the steps, suppleness of the back and engagement of the hind quarters)		2	
Submission (attention and confidence; harmony, lightness and ease of movements; acceptance of the bridle and lightness of the forehand)		2	
Rider's position and seat; correctness and effect of the aids		2	

FURTHER REMARKS:

SUBTOTAL _____

ERRORS (–_____)

TOTAL POINTS _____

Reprinted with permission of AHSA

SECOND LEVEL TEST 4

NEW REQUIREMENTS:
Travers, half turn on haunches

INSTRUCTIONS:
All trot work is done sitting

NO.

		TEST	DIRECTIVE IDEAS	POINTS	COEFFICIENT	TOTAL	REMARKS
1.	A X	Enter collected trot Halt, salute, proceed collected trot	Straightness on center line, transitions, quality of halt and trot				
2.	C MXK K	Track right Medium trot Collected trot	Quality of turn at C, straightness, quality of trots, transitions				
3.	F-B	Shoulder-in left	Quality of trot, execution of movement				
4.	B	Circle left 8m	Quality of trot, roundness and size of circle				
5.	B-M	Travers left	Quality of trot, execution of movement		x2		
6.	HXF F	Medium trot Collected trot	Straightness, quality of trots, transitions				
7.	K-E	Shoulder-in right	Quality of trot, execution of movement				
8.	E	Circle right 8m	Quality of trot, roundness and size of circle				
9.	E-H	Travers right	Quality of trot, execution of movement		x2		
10.	C	Halt, rein back 4 steps, proceed medium walk	Quality of halt and rein back, transitions				
11.	M Between G & H	Turn right Shorten stride and half turn on haunches right, proceed medium walk	Execution of movement		x2		
12.	Between G & M H	Shorten stride and half turn on haunches left, proceed medium walk Turn left	Execution of movement		x2		
13.	S-F F	Free walk on long rein Medium walk	Straightness, quality of walk, transitions		x2		
14.		The medium walk CMG (H) (M) GHS FA	Quality of walk				
15.	A	Collected canter right lead	Calmness and smoothness of depart				
16.	K-H H	Medium canter Collected canter	Straightness, quality of canters, transitions				
17.	C G-E E-B	Down center line Collected canter Half circle 20m, no change of lead	Straightness, quality of canter and counter canter				
18.	B	Simple change of lead	Calmness and smoothness of change				
19.	R	Circle left 10m	Quality of canter, roundness and size of circle				
20.	H-K K	Medium canter Collected canter	Straightness, quality of canters, transitions				
21.	A D-E E-B	Down center line Collected canter Half circle 20m, no change of lead	Straightness, quality of canter and counter canter				
22.	B	Simple change of lead	Calmness and smoothness of change				
23.	P	Circle right 10m	Quality of canter, roundness and size of circle				
24.	F A X	Collected trot Down center line Halt, salute	Straightness on center line, quality of trot and halt, transitions				

Leave arena at free walk on long rein at A

COLLECTIVE MARKS:

Gaits (freedom and regularity)		2	
Impulsion (desire to move forward, elasticity of the steps, suppleness of the back and engagement of the hind quarters)		2	
Submission (attention and confidence; harmony, lightness and ease of movements; acceptance of the bridle and lightness of the forehand)		2	
Rider's position and seat; correctness and effect of the aids		2	

FURTHER REMARKS:

SUBTOTAL _____

ERRORS (–_____)

TOTAL POINTS _____

THIRD LEVEL TEST 1

NEW REQUIREMENTS:
Half pass in trot, half pirouette in walk

INSTRUCTIONS:
All trot work is done sitting

NO.

		TEST	DIRECTIVE IDEAS	POINTS	COEFFICIENT	TOTAL	REMARKS
1.	A / X	Enter collected trot / Halt, salute, proceed collected trot	Straightness on center line, quality of halt and trot, transitions				
2.	C / H-E	Track left / Shoulder-in left	Quality of turn at C, quality of trot, execution of movement				
3.	E / X / B	Turn left / Halt, rein back 4 steps, proceed collected trot / Turn right	Quality of trot, turns, halt, rein back, transitions				
4.	B-F	Shoulder-in right	Quality of trot, execution of movement				
5.	V	Circle right 8m	Quality of trot, roundness and size of circle				
6.	V-I / I / C	Half pass right / Straight ahead / Track right	Quality of trot, execution of movement, straightness on center line		x2		
7.	MXK / K	Medium trot / Collected trot	Straightness, quality of trots, transitions				
8.	P	Circle left 8m	Quality of trot, roundness and size of circle				
9.	P-I / I / C	Half pass left / Straight ahead / Track left	Quality of trot, execution of movement, straightness on center line		x2		
10.	H / Between G & M	Collected walk and turn left / Half pirouette left, proceed collected walk	Execution of movement				
11.	Between G & H / M	Half pirouette right, proceed collected walk / Turn right	Execution of movement				
12.	R-K / K	Extended walk / Collected walk	Straightness, quality of walk, transitions		x2		
13.		The collected walk HG (M) (H) GMR KA	Quality of walk				
14.	A	Collected canter left lead	Calmness and smoothness of depart				
15.	F-M / M	Medium canter / Collected canter	Straightness, quality of canters, transitions				
16.	C-X	Serpentine in 2 loops, width of arena, no change of lead	Quality of canter and counter canter, execution of figure				
17.	X	Circle left 10m	Quality of canter, roundness and size of circle				
18.	X	Simple change of lead	Calmness and smoothness of change				
19.	X	Circle right 10m	Quality of canter, roundness and size of circle				
20.	X-A	Serpentine of 2 loops, width of arena, no change of lead	Quality of counter canter and canter, execution of figure				
21.	K-H / H	Extended canter / Collected canter	Straightness, quality of canters, transitions				
22.	C / MXK / K	Collected trot / Extended trot / Collected trot	Straightness, quality of trots, transitions				
23.	A / X	Down center line / Halt, salute	Straightness on center line, quality of trot and halt, transition				

Leave arena at free walk on long rein at A

COLLECTIVE MARKS:

Gaits (freedom and regularity)		2	
Impulsion (desire to move forward, elasticity of the steps, suppleness of the back and engagement of the hind quarters)		2	
Submission (attention and confidence; harmony, lightness and ease of movements; acceptance of the bridle and lightness of the forehand)		2	
Rider's position and seat; correctness and effect of the aids		2	

FURTHER REMARKS:

SUBTOTAL _____

ERRORS (–_____)

TOTAL POINTS _____

Reprinted with permission of AHSA

THIRD LEVEL TEST 1-S

NEW REQUIREMENTS:
Half pass in trot, half pirouette in walk

INSTRUCTIONS:
All trot work is done sitting

NO.

		TEST	DIRECTIVE IDEAS	POINTS	COEFFICIENT	TOTAL	REMARKS
1.	A X	Enter collected trot Halt, salute, proceed collected trot	Straightness on center line, quality of halt and trot, transitions				
2.	C H-E	Track left Shoulder-in left	Quality of turn at C, quality of trot, execution of movement				
3.	E X B	Turn left Halt, rein back 4 steps, proceed collected trot Turn right	Quality of trot, turns, halt, rein back, transitions				
4.	B-F	Shoulder-in right	Quality of trot, execution of movement				
5.	A	Circle right 8m	Quality of trot, roundness and size of circle				
6.	K-G C	Half pass right Track right	Quality of trot, execution of movement		x2		
7.	MXK K	Medium trot Collected trot	Straightness, quality of trots, transitions				
8.	A	Circle left 8m	Quality of trot, roundness and size of circle				
9.	F-G C	Half pass left Track left	Quality of trot, execution of movement		x2		
10.	H Between G & M	Collected walk and turn left Half pirouette left, proceed collected walk	Execution of movement				
11.	Between G & H M	Half pirouette right, proceed collected walk Turn right	Execution of movement				
12.	B-K K	Extended walk Collected walk	Quality of walks, transitions		x2		
13.		The collected walk	Quality of walk				
14.	A	Collected canter left lead	Calmness and smoothness of depart				
15.	F-M M	Medium canter Collected canter	Straightness, quality of canters, transitions				
16.	C-X	Serpentine in 2 loops, width of arena, no change of lead	Quality of canter and counter canter, execution of figure				
17.	X	Circle left 10m	Quality of canter, roundness and size of circle				
18.	X	Simple change of lead	Calmness and smoothness of change				
19.	X	Circle right 10m	Quality of canter, roundness and size of circle				
20.	X-A	Serpentine of 2 loops, width of arena, no change of lead	Quality of counter canter and canter, execution of figure				
21.	K-H H	Extended canter Collected canter	Straightness, quality of canters, transitions				
22.	C MXK K	Collected trot Extended trot Collected trot	Straightness, quality of trots, transitions				
23.	A X	Down center line Halt, salute	Straightness on center line, quality of trot and halt, transitions				

Leave arena at free walk on long rein at A

COLLECTIVE MARKS:

Gaits (freedom and regularity)		2		
Impulsion (desire to move forward, elasticity of the steps, suppleness of the back and engagement of the hind quarters)		2		
Submission (attention and confidence; harmony, lightness and ease of movement; acceptance of the bridle and lightness of the forehand)		2		
Rider's position and seat; correctness and effect of the aids		2		

FURTHER REMARKS:

SUBTOTAL   _____

ERRORS   (–_____)

TOTAL POINTS   _____

THIRD LEVEL TEST 2

NEW REQUIREMENTS:
Half pass in canter

INSTRUCTIONS:
All trot work is done sitting

NO.

		TEST	DIRECTIVE IDEAS	POINTS	COEFFICIENT	TOTAL	REMARKS
1.	A X	Enter collected trot Halt, salute, proceed collected trot	Straightness on center line, quality of halt and trot, transitions				
2.	C MXK K	Track right Medium trot Collected trot	Quality of turn at C, straightness, quality of trots, transitions				
3.	F-X	Half pass left	Quality of trot, execution of movement				
4.	X X	Circle left 8m Straight ahead	Quality of trot, roundness and size of circle, straightness on center line				
5.	I	Halt, rein back 4 steps, proceed immediately	Quality of halt, rein back, transitions				
6.	I C	Collected canter left lead Track left	Calmness and smoothness of depart, straightness on center line				
7.	H-K K	Medium canter Collected canter	Straightness, quality of canters, transitions				
8.	F-X	Half pass left	Quality of canter, execution of movement		x2		
9.	I I C	Circle left 10m Straight ahead Track left	Quality of canter, roundness and size of circle, straightness on center line				
10.	H SXP P F	Collected walk Extended walk Collected walk Turn right	Quality of walk, transitions, straightness		x2		
11.	Between D & K	Half pirouette right, proceed collected walk	Execution of movement				
12.	Between D & F K	Half pirouette left, proceed collected walk Turn left	Execution of movement				
13.		The collected walk PFD (K) (F) DKA	Quality of walk				
14.	A	Collected canter left lead	Calmness and smoothness of depart				
15.	A-C	Serpentine in 4 loops, width of arena, the first and last loops true canter, the second and third counter canter with a simple change of lead at X	Quality of canter and counter canter, calmness and smoothness of change, execution of figure				
16.	M-F F	Extended canter Collected canter	Straightness, quality of canters, transitions				
17.	K-X	Half pass right	Quality of canter, execution of movement		x2		
18.	I I	Circle right 10m Straight ahead	Quality of canter, roundness and size of circle				
19.	G C HXF F	Collected trot Track left Extended trot Collected trot	Quality of turn, trots, transitions, straightness				
20.	K-X	Half pass right	Quality of trot, execution of movement				
21.	X	Circle right 8m	Quality of trot, roundness and size of circle				
22.	X G	Straight ahead Halt, salute	Straightness on center line, quality of trot and halt, transition				

Leave arena at free walk on long rein at A

COLLECTIVE MARKS:

Gaits (freedom and regularity)				2	
Impulsion (desire to move forward, elasticity of the steps, suppleness of the back and engagement of the hind quarters)				2	
Submission (attention and confidence; harmony, lightness and ease of movements; acceptance of the bridle and lightness of the forehand)				2	
Rider's position and seat; correctness and effect of the aids				2	

FURTHER REMARKS:

SUBTOTAL   _____

ERRORS   (−_____)

TOTAL POINTS   _____

THIRD LEVEL TEST 3

NEW REQUIREMENTS:	INSTRUCTIONS:	NO.
Flying change of lead	All trot work is done sitting	

	TEST	DIRECTIVE IDEAS	POINTS	COEFFICIENT	TOTAL	REMARKS
1.	A — Enter collected canter X — Halt, salute, proceed collected trot	Straightness on center line, transitions, quality of canter, halt and trot				
2.	C — Track left S — Circle left 8m E — Turn left	Quality of turn at C, quality of trot and turn, roundness and size of circle				
3.	B — Turn right P — Circle right 8m	Quality of trot and turn, roundness and size of circle				
4.	V-I — Half pass right I — Straight ahead C — Track right	Quality of trot, execution of movement, straightness on center line				
5.	MXK — Medium trot K — Collected trot	Straightness, quality of trots, transitions				
6.	P-I — Half pass left I — Straight ahead C — Track left	Quality of trot, execution of movement, straightness on center line				
7.	HXF — Extended trot F — Collected trot	Straightness, quality of trots, transitions				
8.	A — Halt, rein back 4 steps, proceed collected walk	Quality of halt and rein back, transitions				
9.	K-R — Extended walk R — Collected walk M — Turn left	Quality of walk, transitions		x2		
10.	Between G & H — Half pirouette left, proceed collected walk	Execution of movement				
11.	Between G & M — Half pirouette right, proceed collected walk H — Turn right	Execution of movement				
12.	The collected walk RMG (H) (M) GHC	Quality of walk				
13.	C — Collected canter right lead	Calmness and smoothness of depart				
14.	M-F — Medium canter F — Collected canter	Straightness, quality of canters, transitions				
15.	A — Down center line D-B — Half pass right	Quality of canter, execution of movement				
16.	Between R & M — Flying change of lead	Calmness and smoothness of change		x2		
17.	H-K — Extended canter K — Collected canter	Straightness, quality of canters, transitions				
18.	A — Down center line D-E — Half pass left	Quality of canter, execution of movement				
19.	Between S & H — Flying change of lead	Calmness and smoothness of change		x2		
20.	C — Collected trot MXK — Extended trot K — Collected trot	Straightness, quality of trots, transitions				
21.	A — Down center line X — Halt, salute	Straightness on center line, quality of trot and halt, transition				

Leave arena at free walk on long rein at A

COLLECTIVE MARKS:

	Gaits (freedom and regularity)			2		
	Impulsion (desire to move forward, elasticity of the steps, suppleness of the back and engagement of the hind quarters)			2		
	Submission (attention and confidence; harmony, lightness and ease of movements; acceptance of the bridle and lightness of the forehand)			2		
	Rider's position and seat; correctness and effect of the aids			2		

FURTHER REMARKS:

SUBTOTAL _____

ERRORS (–_____)

TOTAL POINTS _____

FOURTH LEVEL TEST 1

NEW REQUIREMENTS:
Serpentine in canter with flying
changes of lead

INSTRUCTIONS:
All trot work is done sitting

NO.

		TEST	DIRECTIVE IDEAS	POINTS	COEFFICIENT	TOTAL	REMARKS
1.	A X	Enter collected canter Halt, salute, proceed collected trot	Straightness on center line, quality of canter, halt and trot, transitions				
2.	C MXK K	Track right Extended trot Collected trot	Quality of turn at C, straightness, quality of trots, transitions				
3.	F-B	Shoulder-in left	Quality of trot, execution of movement				
4.	B-G C	Half pass left Track left	Quality of trot, execution of movement				
5.	HXF F	Medium trot, at X 6-7 steps of collected trot (centered at X); proceed medium trot Collected trot	Straightness, quality of trots, transitions				
6.	K-E	Shoulder-in right	Quality of trot, execution of movement				
7.	E-G C	Half pass right Track right	Quality of trot, execution of movement				
8.	MXK K	Extended trot Collected trot	Straightness, quality of trots, transitions				
9.	A L	Down center line Circle left 8m	Straightness on center line, quality of trot, roundness and size of circle				
10.	X	Halt, rein back 4 steps, proceed collected trot	Quality of halt and rein back, transitions				
11.	I C	Circle right 8m Track right	Straightness on center line, quality of trot, roundness and size of circle				
12.	M Between G & H	Collected walk and turn right Half pirouette right	Execution of movement				
13.	Between G & M H	 Half pirouette left Turn left	Execution of movement				
14.	S-F F	Extended walk Collected walk	Straightness, quality of walk, transitions		x2		
15.		The collected walk MG (H) (M) GHS FA	Quality of walk				
16.	A	Collected canter right lead	Calmness and smoothness of depart				
17.	A-C	Serpentine in three loops, width of arena, with flying changes of lead on crossing center line	Quality of canter, execution of figure, calmness and smoothness of changes		x2		
18.	M-F F	Medium canter Collected canter	Straightness, quality of canters, transitions				
19.	A D-B	Down center line Half pass right	Quality of canter, execution of movement				
20.	R	Flying change of lead	Calmness and smoothness of change				
21.	H-K K	Extended canter Collected canter	Straightness, quality of canters, transitions				
22.	A D-E	Down center line Half pass left	Quality of canter, execution of movement				
23.	S	Flying change of lead	Calmness and smoothness of change				
24.	B X G	Turn right Turn right Halt, salute	Quality of canter, turns, halt, transition				

Leave arena at free walk on long rein at A

COLLECTIVE MARKS:

			POINTS	COEFFICIENT	TOTAL	REMARKS
	Gaits (freedom and regularity)			2		
	Impulsion (desire to move forward, elasticity of the steps, suppleness of the back and engagement of the hind quarters)			2		
	Submission (attention and confidence; harmony, lightness and ease of movements; acceptance of the bridle and lightness of the forehand)			2		
	Rider's position and seat; correctness and effect of the aids			2		

FURTHER REMARKS:

SUBTOTAL _____

ERRORS (−_____)

TOTAL POINTS _____

Reprinted with permission of AHSA

FOURTH LEVEL TEST 1-S

NEW REQUIREMENTS:
Serpentine in canter with
flying changes of lead

INSTRUCTIONS:
All trot work is done sitting

NO.

		TEST	DIRECTIVE IDEAS	POINTS	COEFFICIENT	TOTAL	REMARKS
1.	A / X	Enter collected canter / Halt, salute, proceed collected trot	Straightness on center line, quality of canter, halt and trot, transitions				
2.	C / MXK / K	Track right / Extended trot / Collected trot	Quality of turn at C, straightness, quality of trots, transitions				
3.	F-G / C	Half pass left / Track left	Quality of trot, execution of movement				
4.	HXF / F	Medium trot / Collected trot	Straightness, quality of trots, transitions				
5.	K-G / C	Half pass right / Track right	Quality of trot, execution of movement				
6.	MXK / K	Extended trot / Collected trot	Straightness, quality of trots, transitions				
7.	A / Between D & X	Down center line / Circle left 8m	Straightness on center line, quality of trot, roundness and size of circle				
8.	X	Halt, rein back 4 steps, proceed collected trot	Quality of halt, rein back, transitions				
9.	Between X & G / C	Circle right 8m / Track right	Straightness on center line, quality of trot, roundness and size of circle				
10.	M / Between G & H	Collected walk and turn right / Half pirouette right	Execution of movement				
11.	Between G & M / H	Half pirouette left / Turn left	Execution of movement				
12.	E-F / F	Extended walk / Collected walk	Straightness, quality of walks, transitions		x2		
13.		The collected walk	Quality of walk				
14.	A	Collected canter right lead	Calmness and smoothness of depart				
15.	A-C	Serpentine in three loops, width of arena, with flying changes of lead on crossing center line	Quality of canter, execution of figure, calmness and smoothness of changes		x2		
16.	M-F / F	Medium canter / Collected canter	Straightness, quality of canters, transitions				
17.	A / D-M	Down center line / Half pass right	Quality of canter, execution of movement				
18.	C	Flying change of lead	Calmness and smoothness of change				
19.	H-K / K	Extended canter / Collected canter	Straightness, quality of canters, transitions				
20.	A / D-H	Down center line / Half pass left	Quality of canter, execution of movement				
21.	C	Flying change of lead	Calmness and smoothness of change				
22.	B / X / G	Turn right / Turn right / Halt, salute	Straightness on center line, quality of canter, turns, halt, transition				

Leave arena at free walk on long rein at A

COLLECTIVE MARKS:

	POINTS	COEFFICIENT	TOTAL	REMARKS
Gaits (freedom and regularity)		2		
Impulsion (desire to move forward, elasticity of the steps, suppleness of the back and engagement of the hind quarters)		2		
Submission (attention and confidence; harmony, lightness and ease of movements; acceptance of the bridle and lightness of the forehand)		2		
Rider's position and seat; correctness and effect of the aids		2		

FURTHER REMARKS:

SUBTOTAL _____

ERRORS (– _____)

TOTAL POINTS _____

FOURTH LEVEL TEST 2

NEW REQUIREMENTS:
8m circles in canter, flying changes of lead every 4th stride

INSTRUCTIONS:
All trot work is done sitting

NO.

		TEST	DIRECTIVE IDEAS	POINTS	COEFFICIENT	TOTAL	REMARKS
1.	A X	Enter collected canter Halt, salute, proceed collected trot	Straightness on center line, quality of canter, halt, trot, transitions				
2.	C HXF F	Track left Medium trot Collected trot	Quality of turn at C, straightness, quality of trots, transitions				
3.	A	Circle right 8m	Quality of trot, roundness and size of circle				
4.	K-X X-H	Half pass right Half pass left	Quality of trot, execution of movements				
5.	M Between M & R	Collected walk Half pirouette right	Quality of walk, execution of movement				
6.	M	Collected canter left lead	Calmness and smoothness of depart				
7.	H-K K	Medium canter Collected canter	Straightness, quality of canters, transitions				
8.	A L-S	Down center line Half pass left	Quality of canter, straightness on center line, execution of movement				
9.	H	Flying change of lead	Calmness and smoothness of change				
10.	C	Circle right 8m	Quality of canter, roundness and size of circle				
11.	MXK	Change rein, 3 flying changes of lead every fourth stride	Straightness, quality of canter, calmness, smoothness and accuracy of changes		x2		
12.	A	Halt, rein back 4 steps, proceed collected walk	Quality of halt, rein back, transitions				
13.	FPXS S-C	Extended walk Collected walk	Straightness, quality of walk, transitions		x2		
14.		The collected walk AF SC	Quality of walk				
15.	C MXK K	Collected trot Extended trot Collected trot	Straightness, quality of trots, transitions				
16.	A	Circle left 8m	Quality of trot, roundness and size of circle				
17.	F-X X-M	Half pass left Half pass right	Quality of trot, execution of movements				
18.	H Between H & S	Collected walk Half pirouette left	Quality of walk, execution of movement				
19.	H	Collected canter right lead	Calmness and smoothness of depart				
20.	M-F F	Extended canter Collected canter	Straightness, quality of canters, transitions				
21.	A L-R	Down center line Half pass right	Straightness on center line, quality of canter, execution of movement				
22.	M	Flying change of lead	Calmness and smoothness of change				
23.	C	Circle left 8m	Quality of canter, roundness and size of circle				
24.	C HXF F	Collected trot Extended trot Collected trot	Straightness, quality of trots, transitions				
25.	A X	Down center line Halt, salute	Straightness on center line, quality of trot and halt, transition				

Leave arena at free walk on long rein at A

COLLECTIVE MARKS:

Gaits (freedom and regularity)		2		
Impulsion (desire to move forward, elasticity of the steps, suppleness of the back and engagement of the hind quarters)		2		
Submission (attention and confidence; harmony, lightness and ease of movements; acceptance of the bridle and lightness of the forehand)		2		
Rider's position and seat; correctness and effect of the aids		2		

FURTHER REMARKS:

SUBTOTAL _____

ERRORS (−_____)

TOTAL POINTS _____

Reprinted with permission of AHSA

FOURTH LEVEL TEST 3

NEW REQUIREMENTS:
Half pirouettes in canter, flying changes of lead every third stride

INSTRUCTIONS:
All trot work in done sitting

		TEST	DIRECTIVE IDEAS	POINTS	COEFFICIENT	TOTAL	REMARKS
NO.							
1.	A / X	Enter collected canter / Halt, salute, proceed collected trot	Straightness on center line, quality of canter, halt and trot, transitions				
2.	C / MXK / K	Track right / Medium trot / Collected trot	Quality of turn at C, straightness, quality of trots, transitions				
3.	A / D-G / C	Down center line / Three counter-changes of hand in half pass, the 1st half pass to the left and the last to the right of 4m, the other two of 8m / Track right	Quality of trot, execution of movement				
4.	B / X	Turn right / Circle right 8m	Quality of trot and turn, roundness and size of circle				
5.	X / E	Circle left 8m / Turn left	Roundness and size of circle, quality of trot and turn				
6.	FXH / H	Extended trot / Collected trot	Straightness, quality of trots, transitions				
7.	C	Halt, rein back 4 steps, proceed collected walk	Quality of halt and rein back, transitions				
8.	M / Between G & H	Turn right / Half pirouette right, proceed collected walk	Execution of movement				
9.	Between G & M / H	Half pirouette left, proceed collected walk / Turn left	Execution of movement				
10.	S-F / F	Extended walk / Collected walk	Straightness, quality of walk, transitions		x2		
11.		The collected walk CMG (H) (M) GHS FA	Quality of walk				
12.	A	Collected canter right lead	Calmness and smoothness of depart				
13.	KXM / M	Medium canter / Collected canter and flying change of lead	Straightness, quality of canters, transitions, calmness and smoothness of change				
14.	H / Between H & X	Proceed toward X / Half pirouette left	Straightness, quality of canter, execution and placement of movement		x2		
15.	H	Flying change of lead	Calmness and smoothness of change				
16.	M / Between M & X	Proceed toward X / Half pirouette right	Straightness, quality of canter, execution and placement of movement		x2		
17.	M	Flying change of lead	Calmness and smoothness of change				
18.	H-K / K	Extended canter / Collected canter	Straightness, quality of canters, transitions				
19.	A / D-E	Down center line / Half pass left	Quality of canter, execution of movement				
20.	E-B / B	Half circle 20m, no change of lead / Flying change of lead	Quality of counter canter, calmness and smoothness of change				
21.	A / D-B	Down center line / Half pass right	Quality of canter, execution of movement				
22.	B-E / E	Half circle 20m, no change of lead / Flying change of lead	Quality of counter canter, calmness and smoothness of change				
23.	FXH	Change rein, 3 flying changes of lead every fourth stride	Straightness, calmness, smoothness and accuracy of changes				
24.	MXK	Change rein, 3 flying changes of lead every third stride	Straightness, calmness, smoothness and accuracy of changes		x2		
25.	A / X	Down center line / Halt, salute	Straightness on center line, quality of canter, halt, transition				

Leave arena at free walk on long rein at A

COLLECTIVE MARKS:

		Gaits (freedom and regularity)			2		
		Impulsion (desire to move forward, elasticity of the steps, suppleness of the back and engagement of the hind quarters)			2		
		Submission (attention and confidence; harmony, lightness and ease of movements; acceptance of the bridle and lightness of the forehand)			2		
		Rider's position and seat; correctness and effect of the aids			2		

FURTHER REMARKS:

SUBTOTAL _____
ERRORS (−_____)
TOTAL POINTS _____

FIFTH LEVEL TEST 1

NEW REQUIREMENTS:
6m volte in trot

INSTRUCTIONS:
All trot work is done sitting

NO.

		TEST	DIRECTIVE IDEAS	POINTS	COEFFICIENT	TOTAL	REMARKS
1.	A	Enter collected canter	Straightness on center line, quality				
	X	Halt, salute, proceed collected trot	of canter, halt and trot, transitions				
2.	C	Track right	Quality of turn at C,				
	MXK	Medium trot	straightness, quality of				
	K	Collected trot	trots, transitions				
3.	F-X	Half pass left	Quality of trot, execution of movement				
4.	X	Volte left 6m	Quality of trot, roundness and size of circle				
5.	X-G	Shoulder-in left	Execution of movement,				
	C	Track left	quality of trot and turns				
	H	Turn left					
6.	G	Halt, rein back 4 steps, proceed collected trot	Quality of halt, rein back, transitions				
	M	Turn right					
7.	M-F	Medium trot	Straightness, quality of				
	F	Collected trot	trots, transitions				
8.	K-X	Half pass right	Quality of trot, execution of movement				
9.	X	Volte right 6m	Quality of trot, roundness and size of circle				
10.	X-G	Shoulder-in right	Execution of movement,				
	C	Track left	quality of trot and turn				
11.	HXF	Extended trot	Straightness, quality of				
	F	Collected trot	trots, transitions				
12.	A	Medium walk	Quality of walk				
13.	KVXRM	Extended walk	Straightness, quality of	x2			
	M	Collected walk	walks, transitions				
	H	Turn left					
14.	Between G & M	Half pirouette left	Execution of movement				
15.	Between G & H	Half pirouette right	Execution of movement				
16.		The collected walk	Quality of walk				
17.	G	Collected canter right lead	Calmness and smoothness of depart				
	M	Turn right					
18.	M-F	Medium canter	Straightness, quality of				
	F	Collected canter	canters, transitions				
19.	K-X	Half pass right	Quality of canter, execution				
	X	Flying change of lead	of movements, calmness and				
	X-H	Half pass left	smoothness of changes				
	H	Flying change of lead					
20.	H-M-X	Collected canter	Quality of canter, execution				
	Between		and placement of movement,				
	M & X	Half pirouette right	calmness and smoothness of				
	M	Flying change of lead	change	x2			
21.	M-H-X	Collected canter	Quality of canter, execution				
	Between		and placement of movement,				
	H & X	Half pirouette left	calmness and smoothness of				
	H	Flying change of lead	change	x2			
22.	MXK	5 flying changes of lead every fourth stride	Straightness, calmness, smoothness and accuracy of changes				
23.	FXH	5 flying changes of lead every third stride	Straightness, calmness, smoothness and accuracy of changes	x2			
24.	MXK	Extended canter	Straightness, quality of				
	K	Collected canter and flying change of lead	canters, transitions, calmness and smoothness of change				
25.	A	Down center line	Straightness on center line,				
	X	Halt, salute	quality of canter, halt, transition				

Leave arena at free walk on long rein at A

COLLECTIVE MARKS:

Gaits (freedom and regularity)			2			
Impulsion (desire to move forward, elasticity of the steps, suppleness of the back and engagement of the hind quarters)			2			
Submission (attention and confidence; harmony, lightness and ease of movements; acceptance of the bridle and lightness of the forehand)			2			
Rider's position and seat; correctness and effect of the aids			2			

FURTHER REMARKS:

SUBTOTAL _____

ERRORS (–_____)

TOTAL POINTS _____

Reprinted with permission of AHSA

FIFTH LEVEL TEST 2

NEW REQUIREMENTS:
"Swing," pirouettes in canter, flying changes of lead every 2nd stride

INSTRUCTIONS:
All trot work is done sitting

NO.

		TEST	DIRECTIVE IDEAS	POINTS	COEFFICIENT	TOTAL	REMARKS
1.	A X	Enter collected canter Halt, salute, proceed collected trot	Straightness on center line, quality of canter, halt, trot, transitions				
2.	C HXF F	Track left Medium trot Collected trot	Quality of turn at C, straightness, quality of trots, transitions				
3.	A D-G C	Down center line 4 counter changes of hand in half pass, the first half pass to the right and the last to the right of 3m, the other 3 of 6m Track left	Quality of trot, execution of movement				
4.	E X B	Turn left Halt, rein back 4 steps, forward 4 steps, rein back 4 steps, proceed immediately in collected trot Turn right	Quality of trot and turns, execution of movement, transitions				
5.	KXM M	Extended trot Collected trot	Straightness, quality of trots, transitions				
6.	C H Between G & M	Collected walk Turn left Half pirouette left	Execution of movement				
7.	Between G & H	Half pirouette right	Execution of movement				
8.	G-M-R-E E	Extended walk Collected walk	Straightness, quality of walks, transitions		x2		
9.		The collected walk	Quality of walk				
10.	V	Collected canter left lead	Calmness and smoothness of depart				
11.	A D-G C	Down center line 3 counter-changes of hand in half pass to the left and right of the center line, the first half pass to the left and the last to the right of 4 strides, the two others of 8 strides finishing on the right lead Track right	Quality of canter, execution of movement				
12.	MXK K	Medium canter Collected canter and flying change of lead	Straightness, quality of canters, calmness and smoothness of change				
13.	FXH Between F & X X	Change rein Pirouette left Flying change of lead	Straightness, quality of canter, execution and placement of movement, calmness and smoothness of change		x2		
14.	Between X & H	Pirouette right	Straightness, quality of canter, execution and placement of movement		x2		
15.	MXK	7 flying changes of lead every third stride	Straightness, calmness, smoothness and accuracy of changes				
16.	F-M M	Extended canter Collected canter	Straightness, quality of canters, transitions				
17.	HXF	7 flying changes of lead every second stride	Straightness, calmness, smoothness and accuracy of changes		x2		
18.	A X	Down center line Halt, rein back 4 steps, proceed collected canter right lead	Straightness on center line, quality of canter, halt, rein back, transitions				
19.	G	Halt, salute	Quality of halt				

Leave arena at free walk on long rein at A

COLLECTIVE MARKS:

Gaits (freedom and regularity)		2		
Impulsion (desire to move forward, elasticity of the steps, suppleness of the back and engagement of the hind quarters)		2		
Submission (attention and confidence; harmony, lightness and ease of movements; acceptance of the bridle and lightness of the forehand)		2		
Rider's position and seat; correctness and effect of the aids		2		

FURTHER REMARKS:

SUBTOTAL _____

ERRORS (–_____)

TOTAL POINTS _____

Reprinted with permission of AHSA

FIFTH LEVEL TEST 3

NEW REQUIREMENTS:
Flying changes of lead every stride, piaffe, passage

INSTRUCTIONS:
All trot work is done sitting

NO.

#		TEST	DIRECTIVE IDEAS	POINTS	COEFFICIENT	TOTAL	REMARKS
1.	A / X	Enter collected canter / Halt, salute, proceed collected trot	Straightness on center line, quality of canter, halt, trot, transitions				
2.	C / MXK / K	Track right / Extended trot / Collected trot	Quality of turn at C, straightness, quality of trots, transitions				
3.	F-E	Half pass left	Quality of trot, execution of movement				
4.	E-M	Half pass right	Quality of trot, execution of movement				
5.	H-P / P	Medium trot / Collected trot	Quality of trots, transitions				
6.	Between P & F	Proceed in passage to A	Quality, cadence, regularity				
7.	A	Piaffe 7-8 steps (1m forward permitted) Proceed immediately in collected trot	Quality, cadence, regularity				
8.		Transitions from passage to piaffe and from piaffe to collected trot					
9.	A-K / K-R / R	Collected trot / Extended trot / Collected trot and immediately collected walk	Quality of trots, transitions				
10.	RMC	Collected walk	Quality of walk				
11.	C	Piaffe 7-8 steps (1m forward permitted) Proceed immediately in passage	Quality, cadence, regularity				
12.	C-H	Passage	Quality, cadence, regularity				
13.		Transitions from collected walk to piaffe and piaffe to passage					
14.	Between H & S / S / I / R	Collected trot / Turn left / Collected canter right / Turn right	Quality of trot, canter, transition and turns				
15.	BLK / L	Change rein / Pirouette right	Straightness, execution and placement of movement		x2		
16.	K / KAF	Flying change of lead / Collected canter	Calmness and smoothness of change, quality of canter				
17.	FLE / L	Change rein / Pirouette left	Straightness, execution and placement of movement		x2		
18.	E / S	Flying change of lead / Turn right	Calmness and smoothness of change, quality of turn				
19.	I / R	Halt, rein back 4 steps, forward 4 steps, rein back 4 steps, proceed immediately in collected canter left / Turn left	Quality of halt, submission in "swing", quality of rein back, canter, turn				
20.		Transitions from collected canter to halt and from rein back to collected canter					
21.	CHP	Extended walk	Straightness, quality of walk		x2		
22.	P	Collected walk	Quality of walk				
23.	A / KXM	Collected canter right / 9 flying changes of lead every second stride	Straightness, calmness, smoothness and accuracy of changes				
24.	HXF / F	Extended canter / Collected canter and flying change of lead	Quality of canters, transitions, calmness and smoothness of change				
25.	A / D-G / C	Down center line / 3 counter-changes of hand in half pass to either side of the center line with flying changes of lead at each change of direction, the first half pass to the right and the last to the left of 4 strides, the two others of 8 strides finishing on the left lead / Track left	Quality of canter, execution of movement				
26.	HXF	7 flying changes of lead every stride	Straightness, calmness, smoothness and accuracy of changes		x2		
27.	A / X	Down center line / Halt, salute	Straightness on center line, quality of canter, halt, transition				

Leave arena at free walk on long rein at A

COLLECTIVE MARKS:

		POINTS	COEFFICIENT	TOTAL	REMARKS
	Gaits (freedom and regularity)		2		
	Impulsion (desire to move forward, elasticity of the steps, suppleness of the back and engagement of the hind quarters)		2		
	Submission (attention and confidence; harmony, lightness and ease of movements; acceptance of the bridle and lightness of the forehand)		2		
	Rider's position and seat; correctness and effect of the aids		2		

FURTHER REMARKS:

SUBTOTAL   _____
ERRORS   (− _____)
TOTAL POINTS   _____

Reprinted with permission of AHSA

FIFTH LEVEL TEST 4

INSTRUCTIONS:
All trot work is done sitting

NO.

		TEST	DIRECTIVE IDEAS	POINTS	COEFFICIENT	TOTAL	REMARKS
1.	A / X	Enter collected canter Halt, salute, proceed collected trot	Straightness on center line, quality of canter, halt, trot, transitions				
2.	C / HXF / F	Track left Extended trot Collected trot	Straightness, quality of trots, transitions				
3.	K-B	Half pass right	Quality of trot, execution of movement				
4.	B-H	Half pass left	Quality of trot, execution movement				
5.	MXK / K	Extended trot Collected trot	Straightness, quality of trots, transitions				
6.	F	Collected walk	Quality of walk				
7.	PXS	Extended walk	Straightness, quality of walk		x2		
8.	S / H	Collected walk Turn right	Quality of walk				
9.	GMBX	Passage	Quality, cadence, regularity				
10.	X	Piaffe 10-12 steps	Quality, cadence, regularity				
11.	XEV	Passage	Quality, cadence, regularity				
12.		The transitions between passage and piaffe					
13.	V	Collected canter	Calmness and smoothness of depart				
14.	A D-G C	Down center line Five counter-changes of hand in half pass to either side of the center line with flying changes of lead at each change of direction, the first half pass to the left and the last to the right of 3 strides, the four others of 6 strides finishing on the right lead Track right	Quality of canter, execution of movement				
15.	MXK / K	Extended canter Collected canter and flying change of lead	Straightness, quality of canters, transitions, calmness and smoothness of change				
16.	A Between D & L X	Down center line Pirouette left Flying change of lead	Straightness, quality of canter, execution and placement of movement, calmness and smoothness of change		x2		
17.	Between I & G C	Pirouette right Track right	Straightness, quality of canter, execution and placement of movement		x2		
18.	MXK	9 flying changes of lead every second stride	Straightness, calmness, smoothness and accuracy of changes				
19.	FXH	15 flying changes of lead every stride	Straightness, calmness, smoothness and accuracy of changes		x2		
20.	C / MBXI	Collected trot Passage	Quality of trot and passage, cadence and regularity				
21.	I	Piaffe 10-12 steps	Quality, cadence, regularity				
22.	I-G	Passage	Quality, cadence, regularity				
23.		The transitions between passage and piaffe					
24.	G	Halt, salute	Quality of halt, transition				

Leave arena at free walk on long rein at A

COLLECTIVE MARKS:

Gaits (freedom and regularity)		2	
Impulsion (desire to move forward, elasticity of the steps, suppleness of the back and engagement of the hind quarters)		2	
Submission (attention and confidence; harmony, lightness and ease of movements; acceptance of the bridle and lightness of the forehand)		2	
Rider's position and seat; correctness and effect of the aids		2	

FURTHER REMARKS:

SUBTOTAL _____

ERRORS (−_____)

TOTAL POINTS _____